VN

2

i

The Proactive Manager

THE PROACTIVE MANAGER

THE COMPLETE BOOK OF PROBLEM SOLVING AND DECISION MAKING

LORNE C. PLUNKETT

GUY A. HALE
The Alamo Consulting Group

A Wiley-Interscience Publication
JOHN WILEY & SONS

New York • Chichester • Brisbane • Toronto • Singapore

Library of Congress Cataloging in Publication Data:

Plunkett, Lorne C.
    The proactive manager.

71423

    "A Wiley-Interscience publication."
    Bibliography: p.
    Includes index.
    1. Management.   2.   Problem solving.   3.   Decision-
making.   4.   Corporate planning.   I.   Hale, Guy A.
II.   Title.
HD31.P53   658.4'03   81-11382
ISBN 0-471-08509-X   AACR2

Printed in the United States of America

10 9 8 7 6 5 4 3 2 1

To those who strive for excellence and freedom from the irrational

Preface

A fter having worked as industrial management consultants specializing in management development for a total of 25 years, we felt there was a strong need for an up-to-date and complete book on problem solving, decision making, and planning. It has been difficult for the manager or individual to find this information in a single, clear presentation. The subjects of Problem Solving and Decision Making have been presented to the public in a confusing manner. There are over 100 books in the Library of Congress on these topics, and most of them present only parts of these processes. Therefore, it is our objective to present managers with a tool that represents the state of the art—a useful book that managers will refer to over and over again.

This book is a readable, precise presentation of structured, systematic mental processes. These processes will simplify and make more effective problem solving, decision making, and planning for managers. In addition, we blend the creative and rational approaches to problem solving and decision making and planning. Heretofore, authors of the rational approach have denied or ignored the need for creative problem solving skills, and the creative practitioners have fought or denied the need for structured mental processes for individuals or groups. Thousands of managers are trained every year in both disciplines with no guidance as to how they complement each other.

In addition to combining the structured and creative processes, we present some true experiences of how the application of our processes within client companies has saved millions of dollars. The names and locations of the companies have been disguised to protect the privacy and the confidentiality of the professional working relationship.

For serious students of the problem solving, decision making, and planning models we present, there is a case study at the end of each basic

vii

chapter. These case studies allow individuals to test their understanding of the processes presented. Case resolutions are provided in the Appendix.

The skills presented in this book are equally valuable to the line supervisor in industry, the student of management, and the chief executive officer of an international operation. Each has a need to find the root cause of his or her problems, to choose the best possible course of action when making a decision, and to assure that decisions will have the highest probability of succeeding. This book will strengthen these abilities for every reader.

GUY A. HALE
LORNE PLUNKETT

Walnut Creek, California
September 1981

Acknowledgments

We gratefully acknowledge the valuable involvement of several individuals who have enhanced the quality of this book by their helpful suggestions and ideas. Many people have in so many ways made significant contributions; however, we would especially like to thank the following: Robert E. Benjamin, Diane Dias, Sandra Dougherty, Jerold W. Farnsworth, Herb Gabora, J. D. Garner, Diane Plunkett, Rosalie Pryor, and Eric Rees.

G. A. H.
L. C. P.

Contents

The Proactive Manager

Introduction

"*To be or not to be, that is the question.*" While not all choices managers face have the life or death implications that Hamlet's did, dealing effectively with uncertainty is crucial to modern management. Uncertainty is defined as a set of circumstances providing the manager with no obvious answer but, nevertheless, requiring resolution. Obviously, this definition applies to most managerial activities. In most organizations, managerial performance is measured by the effective identification and resolution of uncertainty.

In modern management, uncertainty is an inescapable part of the environment within which managers work; no manager can avoid it. Since uncertainty is inevitable, successful managers must learn to "manage the effects of uncertainty." One of the difficulties of controlling the results of uncertainty is that it takes so many forms. These forms represent major challenges for management. As long as management is carried out by people and involves change, the skill of analyzing uncertainty will not become obsolete. In this book we explore four distinct kinds of uncertainty and a process for handling each one.

WHAT DO WE MEAN BY PROCESS?

Process is a prescribed sequence of activities that sequentially and logically relate to each other to achieve a predetermined objective. It can more simply be described as the activity that converts input to output. In the manufacturing or industrial environment, the process is the means of converting raw material to a finished product. In management terms, it is the application of logic, judgment, and information analysis. For a process to be identifiable, it must have a prescribed sequence that is proved by results to be repeatable. It must be capable of being labeled and transmitted. It must be independent of the variable experiences of the manager.

1

The word "process" has been adopted by the behaviorists in management. They use the word to describe the interpersonal action that occurs in managerial situations. This usage is as accurate as ours; it simply describes a different application of the term. Edgar Schein, in his book *Process Consultation*, notes that any group is concerned with at least six different processes, one of them being that of Problem Solving and Decision Making. It is this process that we address here. It is in no way a denial of the other processes. It is a determination based on our experience of where we produce the maximum impact on managerial effectiveness.

WHAT IS PROACTIVE MANAGEMENT?

We use the term Proactive Management to describe a set of analytical skills used to resolve the uncertainties facing managers. The skills or processes are different for each different form of uncertainty. Perhaps the easiest method of classifying the processes is the use of a time frame. A manager has several basic time frames to manage:

1. *The Past.* Managers exist in a sea of events that are products of the past. Where we are today is a cumulative effect of earlier events. When charting directions for the present and future, the manager must understand why certain things happened. The process applied to this need for understanding is called Cause Analysis. Key questions include "Why did it happen?" and "What caused the situation to get to this point?"

2. *The Present.* Managers live in the present and need to control the events current in their areas of responsibility. They have a conscious need to react appropriately, make decisions, and assess events to ensure that desired results are achieved. This process necessarily involves different steps because the input and end result are different. The process for this set of requirements is called Decision Making. The central question is "Where do we go from here?"

3. *The Future.* Managers are becoming more and more concerned about directing future events and performance. The emphasis on proactive skills rather than reactive skills is increasing in most effective organizations. The ability to implement a plan successfully is becoming as important as the ability to develop the plan. The plan implementation activities are included in the process of Plan Analysis. Critical questions are "What will happen as we progress toward our goal?" and "How can we ensure the success of our plan?"

4. *Past, Present, and Future All Together.* While a time frame classification is useful, it is not always realistic because many concerns are a result of "scrambled" events. In these situations, managers are faced with a conglomerate of concerns that appear to exist in all three time

Figure I.1   Interrelationship of proactive management skills.

frames. In these instances, managers must assess the situation to know where and how to begin resolution. The process used is called Situation Review and the outcome of this process is a detailed list of priorities requiring managerial response.

Proactive Management is all of these processes. Each has a different focus and sequence of steps. Each set of skills must be applied separately and sequentially; however, the processes are interrelated (as shown in Figure I.1). A manager could enter the cycle at any process and then follow a logical progression. For example, if a manager entered the cycle at Cause Analysis, finding the cause of a problem would normally lead to a decision regarding the proper fix or corrective action. Similarly, if Decision Making were the entry point, it seems reasonable to believe that the decision made would then be successfully implemented. And, finally, plans developed and implemented frequently go off track, requiring Cause Analysis for restoration.

In this book we begin the discussion of the Proactive Manager with Cause Analysis and then follow the cycle through to Situation Review, as outlined in Figure I.2.

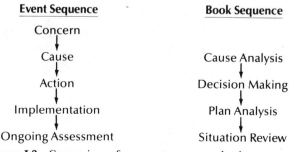

Figure I.2   Comparison of process sequence to book sequence.

WHY MANAGE PROACTIVELY?

Any manager who survives in an organization today is using some form of structured process. Some managers do it consciously and do it well. Some managers do it unconsciously and they, too, do it well. Then there are the other managers who go throughout their careers reacting to situations rather than managing proactively.

Our attempt is to increase awareness of the rational processes. A competent manager might ask "Isn't it good enough that I solve my problems?" and "Why is it important to know *how* I solve them?" The answers to these questions are critical to this book.

There are at least six valid reasons why increasing a manager's level of consciousness pays off:

1. *Development of Subordinates.* How can managers develop their employees' logic if they themselves do not have a clear, conscious picture of the steps they go through and have the ability to communicate their method to others?

    "Do as you see me doing, because I can't conceptualize what I do."

2. *Selling Ideas.* In most situations, we are not in the luxurious position of being able to act without first convincing someone else it is worthwhile. Brilliant flashes of insight are frequently misunderstood and hence rejected by others who may not appreciate how the solution was reached.

    "Trust me, I know I'm right."

3. *Time Management.* Many situations requiring some form of analysis are not resolved in a single sitting. Frequently, we have to put them aside while we wait for data or defer them to deal with an emergency. Without a designated approach, we would have to start at the beginning every time we returned to the concern.

    "I know I was doing something important."

    "Maybe my secretary knows where I left off."

4. *Confidence.* If a conscious approach has been used to resolve a situation, a manager knows that all the bases have been covered and that there is a good likelihood of his or her being correct. Although we have observed some excellent "Eureka" results, there is no attempt here to guarantee an improvement in the quality of everyone's rational processes. Nevertheless, it is critical to sharpen the manager's existing skill.

    "I hope they don't ask me any questions; there are too many holes!"

5. *Replication.* A manager's experience is useful only if it can be projected into future activity. A conscious process of problem

solving allows a manager to duplicate that application when similar situations occur. Not every situation has to be approached on a trial and error basis without the benefit of being able to apply past successes.

"Let me see . . . how did I fix it before?"

"I sure wish I knew which approach worked well last time."

"Oh well . . . here goes!"

6. *Structured Analysis in Groups.*   Most managers need to apply rational skills as members of one or more working groups. It might be as the boss, a member of a committee, or a subordinate. We all have developed our concepts of rational thinking based on the experiences we have had as individuals. Those experiences are different for each one of us. It is not surprising then that our rational processes are not necessarily the same. For example, if we took five managers, put them in separate rooms, and asked them to solve the same problems, we would not expect the same results. Likewise, if we put these five managers in one room, we should not expect a sudden merging of rational processes. Each manager would still apply logic (as he or she defines it) to the resolution of the problem.

"Does anybody have any idea how we might resolve this decision?"

These six reasons provide a sound rationale for a careful review of Proactive Management, a systematic method of information processing.

The process of logic is simply the application of common sense.

HOW DID PROACTIVE MANAGEMENT DEVELOP?

Individual Contributions

PLATO

While much early Greek philosophy focused on moral and ethical issues, there are traces of concern for rationality interspersed in the literature. In *The Republic*, Plato argues convincingly for the development of Philosopher Kings and stresses scientific and rational skills as critical to leadership in the ideal state. Unfortunately, the effect of rationality was overwhelmed by the effects of palace intrigues and family jealousies.

Through Plato we are also exposed to some of the earliest references to logical thought. His writings on Socrates and the development of the Socratic method outline fundamental principles in the management of uncertainty. Socrates focused on several elements of the currently accepted thinking process. Specifically, he developed the concept of stating and accepting propositions and then testing their validity through the extension of their consequences. This is exactly the process of causal testing that occurs daily in any business enterprise. In addition to describing this concept, he also pointed out the danger of confusing the testing of the cause with the proof of its validity. Even today, the gathering of facts is often confused with proof of causality.

DAVID HUME

While many intervening philosophers (e.g., Bacon, Newton, and John Stuart Mill) could be mentioned, a major contributor to the development of logic was David Hume. His paper *Causality* in 1739–1740 introduced the elements of cause and effect relationships that still permeate today's management practices. Hume introduced three principles of causality that still apply. To understand cause and effect, which is the basis of uncertainty, it is critical to define the requirements of a cause. To be verified, a cause must have three characteristics:

1. *Cause is inevitable.* The cause will inevitably produce a particular effect. Whenever that cause operates, the effect is always present. When the effect is present the cause will be present too.
2. *Cause is positive.* There is a direct cause/effect relationship. The cause has the capacity to actually create a specified effect.
3. *Cause/effect is immediate.* The cause/effect is a direct connection. Action through a second cause is not required.

Hume also developed "Hume's Skepticism," the idea that all people (i.e., managers) should suspend belief in a cause/effect relationship until it is empirically proven and fits the three requirements previously noted. Essentially, he is providing the manager with the philosophical basis to question cause/effect relationships. Such caution is critical to good problem solving and decision making. While overuse of Hume's skepticism may result in infinite delays, underuse may result in costly actions that have no chance of success, high-priced "over fixes" and expensive trial and error decision making.

CHESTER BARNARD

The next important reference point is Barnard. Management, unlike philosophy, does not have a long literary history. Early writers like Taylor, Fayol, and Galbraith began only after the turn of the century. The initial work in this field bridges philosophy with management, focusing on the application of philosophy to business. Barnard's book, *Functions of the Executive* (1935), is different; it concentrates on the skills required to be an effective executive. The author presents basic logic and judgement as the key prerequisites for success in management. A range of management writers have since been influenced by his work.

HERBERT SIMON

One important writer who acknowledges the impact of Barnard on management theory is Herbert Simon. His book, *Administrative Behavior* (1945), is a landmark in decision making. One significant principle Simon originated is the concept of "weighted criteria evaluation," a technique for considering values relatively. Based on his 1945 text and other accomplishments, Simon was awarded the 1979 Nobel Prize for Economics.

IRWIN J. D. BROSS

In his book, *Design for Decision* (1953), Bross describes the historical development of human beings in terms of which societal classes have been delegated the right of decision making. In his terms, historical development can be understood if we study the practice of rational processes by these classes. The author dramatically shows the need for handling uncertainty by studying decision makers from the priests of ancient Egypt to modern politicians and civil servants.

CHARLES KEPNER AND BENJAMIN TREGOE

Perhaps the most conscious attempt to take the developing concepts of cause/effect analysis and decision making occurs in *The Rational Manager* (1965) by Kepner and Tregoe. Their work was the first attempt to marry logic to business practices and probably has had the most significant impact on management. Their book formulates practical tools using these concepts so that day-to-day management can be made consistent with accepted principles of logic.

HENRY MINTZBERG

In *The Nature of Managerial Work* (1973) Mintzberg presents a new and exciting set of challenges to the traditional role of executives as problem solvers, decision makers, and planners. His emphasis on what managers *really do* versus what they *think they do* is a stepping stone for the further development of management theory. In the final analysis, managers will still have to process information. How well that is done will determine their ultimate effectiveness.

Organizational Responses

While theorists have developed more complex concepts about uncertainty, organizations have developed some very pragmatic reactions to the same. The response patterns presented here illustrate different reactions to uncertainty. All are currently in use in various organizations today.

SYSTEMS APPROACH

In this approach to structuring uncertainty, an organization creates a complex set of standard operating procedures. The primary purpose of this approach is to reduce the discretionary responsibilities of individuals until uncertainty no longer exists. This orientation is frequently observed in either highly decentralized operations or in older, hierarchical companies. An attempt is made to predict both the characteristics of and the range of appropriate responses to any and every given situation. From an organization's viewpoint, this approach requires a tremendous investment in the development and maintenance of procedures.

As long as practices, problems, and issues remain constant, this approach will function effectively. Decision making is generally restricted to the elite few at the top. Rapid turnover and poor motivation are predictable results of an organization that depends on systems for answers to uncertainty.

UPWARD DELEGATION APPROACH

Another organization response to uncertainty is to establish an operating policy that requires all uncertain situations to be referred to higher-level managers. In this approach, there is an heroic assumption that the higher the level of management, the greater the capability. While in many instances this is true, it does violate many accepted rules of good problem solving. One of these guidelines is that a problem is best solved at that level in the organization where the most information and experience reside.

The smaller the organization the more feasible this approach. In larger structures, there is a disproportionate amount of responsibility and work given to a few higher-level people. Organizational members at lower levels frequently seek other employment opportunities because of the demeaning role they must accept.

SKILL DEVELOPMENT APPROACH

We believe the most effective approach is to consciously develop the skills and abilities of managers to proactively anticipate and manage the effects of uncertainty. Good management combines the rational/logical processes with various other qualities necessary for effectiveness. If an organization intentionally recognizes, develops, and provides rewards for rational approaches, it will begin to manage uncertainty more effectively. When managers at all levels feel they can "handle the situation," uncertainty tends to lose its threatening characteristics. Indeed, uncertainty becomes a challenge and an opportunity rather than a threat.

This approach assumes that skills, once developed, will be exercised. It assumes that uncertainty is accepted as part of reality and that people must use skills to manage it. It also assumes that proactive rational skills can be taught and learned. Based on many years' experience in this approach, we believe these skills are not only transferable but are the cornerstone for all management development.

Great problem solvers are not born . . . they learn how to probe and respond. Great decision makers are not born . . . they learn how to evaluate, assess, and decide. These assumptions and skill development processes will be discussed in the section, "Developing Proactive Skills in Others."

PROACTIVE SKILLS

This section of the book describes in depth the concepts that underlie proactive management. The discussion of each analytical process is given a separate chapter and generally follows a pattern of (1) concept description, (2) case study, (3) application example, (4) concept variations in Cause Analysis and Decision Making, and (5) flowchart and worksheet.

The length of the chapters is more reflective of the complexity of the concept theme than of the importance of each process. We present a basic set of working skills that managers can refer to and use daily. To give the reader an idea of how each process can be used, we include a sampling of various client situations we have worked on. These application examples are presented to show how the process has been used in the "real world" and will, it is hoped, trigger in the reader's mind some valuable ideas for practical use. The case studies are for readers to test their understanding of the concepts. The sample analyses that reflect our solutions are included in the Appendix.

CHAPTER 1

Cause Analysis

In introducing Cause Analysis, it is critical to keep the concept in proper perspective with regard to a manager's need to achieve results. The stimulus for managers to concern themselves with historical analysis is created by present events. A manager lives in a constant struggle with the laws of cause and effect. When the "effects" have built up to a point where they require action, involved managers have to locate their position in the cause/effect chain. If the effects that require attention are undesirable, unexpected, and cannot be easily explained, managers can utilize Cause Analysis as a tool. But they must do so in a manner consistent with their goals. Managers cannot afford the luxury of analyzing for cause simply for the intellectual challenge involved. Goals must be maintained (or expanded) when unforeseen effects disrupt the work effort.

This is not always as easy as it sounds. While it is easy to recognize the "big problem" when it arises, it is often the little, rather insidious ones that (because of their cumulative nature) create the most intolerable situations. Consider the plight of the experimental frog in the laboratory. A beaker of water is heated to the boiling point and then the frog is dropped into the beaker. The frog reacts so violently that, more often than not, it jumps out of the beaker, effectively removing itself from the steaming liquid. If, however, one places the frog in the beaker first and then slowly increases the temperature, it swims around until it dies.

Basically, a manager has three options when undesirable effects become visible: (1) fix it, (2) buy time and fix it later, or (3) adapt to the new situation. In this reactive mode, the manager must determine which of these actions to choose. We concern ourselves with the first—"Fix it." We cover the other two when we look at Decision Making functions.

If a manager decides that correcting the situation is appropriate, there are two sound responses:

1. I know why it is happening and, therefore, it is only a question of choosing an appropriate action.

2. I am not sure why it is happening and, therefore, I must analyze the problem prior to fixing it.

There is of course a third reaction which, unfortunately, is all too prevalent, and it is:

3. I *think* I know the cause and, therefore, I will take an action.

The impact of this reaction is that trial and error takes precedence over conscious analysis. Every "intuitive hunch" yields another response and that can lead to a waste of energy and resources. As "fix" gets piled upon "fix," the true situation tends to get fuzzier and thus more difficult to resolve.

The correct definition of the word "fix" means to remove the cause. If you have a problem with your sales staff because they are not filing their reports on time or correctly, the only hope of resolving that problem is to find the cause of the delays or errors and deal with it. Unfortunately, many times a "shotgun" approach is used. "If I fix enough things, I will ultimately remove the cause." That approach is expensive, however, due to the cost of "overfix" and time-consumption. If a problem warrants resolution, it follows that it deserves a logical, analytical approach, which will reduce trial and error and provide a single action for resolution. When confronted with mechanical problems on an automobile, we frequently pay the price of the local mechanic whose problem-solving process involves starting at the fan belt and working back, changing parts along the way. While eventually the problem is resolved, our bank accounts usually suffer.

In Cause Analysis, it is useful to think of the problem as an iceberg—what you see only hints at the entirety of the problem. Only through analysis can a manager determine its actual size and scope. Being aware of this iceberg phenomenon, most managers try to better understand the problem at hand by collecting more data. Then managers may be able to see the whole "iceberg." Managers may, however, still be unable to deal with it unless they can classify the data into a useful format—separating the relevant from the irrelevant. They don't need to collect data on the entire "Polar Cap" in order to put a particular iceberg into proper focus. One of the most common mistakes managers make in this task is confusing Symptoms, Causes, and Effects.

The following definitions help resolve this issue:

Symptoms	These are the visible parts of the problem that bring it to your attention. Symptoms never explain a problem—they are only manifestations.

Causes	Causes are the verifiable stimuli that make something happen. These are the reasons for effects.
Effects	These represent the impact of the problem. Effects trigger a need to resolve the problem. Symptoms are part of the effects.

For example:

Symptom	Frequent headaches.
Cause	Eyestrain.
Effect	Loss of productivity at school.

Symptoms are useful as they provide the first clues that there is a problem. In some instances, the symptoms may require attention before the real problem is resolved. For example, if a headache gets severe enough, it will require medication for relief, even if the doctor realizes that the headache is only a symptom of the real problem.

Likewise, if "grumbling," "tardiness," or "absenteeism" begin to appear in an organization, effective managers recognize that these may be only symptoms of a more fundamental problem. They should recognize that managing the situation effectively may require taking action on the symptoms, at the same time realizing that this action will not remove the cause of the problem. Further action will be required later to deal with and "fix" the cause.

Dealing with symptoms, as illustrated above, is normal and effective management, provided that managers do not delude themselves by thinking they are solving the problem. In reality, they are only buying time. If they don't deal with the cause of the problem itself, it will only reappear in the same or a different form at another time.

The effective problem solver looks for two things when dealing with symptoms:

1. If this symptom (problem) is dealt with, will there be any need for further action? If the answer is yes, then only a symptom is being dealt with.

2. Do I need to know the cause to resolve this effectively? If the answer is yes, then action to relieve the symptom may only buy time.

Once immersed in the analysis of data, an effective problem solver looks for:

1. A causal chain—this is a cause/effect hierarchy that will lead backward (from effect to cause) to a point where action that will resolve

the situation can be taken. This chain is explored further at the end of this chapter.

At each step in the cause/effect chain, the problem solver must be absolutely sure that the cause is real and not hypothetical. A rule of thumb is, "If in doubt, stop and find the cause." The only cost will be time and the benefit of increased confidence is usually well worth it. Truly effective problem solving leads to the resolution of the underlying causes. Thus, the search for underlying causes is critical.

2. A separation of the several apparent problems to effectively focus on the most critical problem, rather than diffuse efforts by handling a myriad of interrelated problems.

For Cause Analysis purposes, we identify three characteristics that must exist before such formal action is taken:

1. There must be visible, undesirable effects; that is, something unexpected must be happening.
2. The effects must be sufficiently out of phase with what was expected, to warrant some analysis.
3. Causes need to be known for a proper reaction to these effects.

Every problem-solving process we have reviewed agrees with the principle that the first step of resolution is "clear understanding." To *define* the concern clearly and properly is to begin the resolution. The following quotes illustrate this concept:

> The "should" of the situation, minus the "actual" of the situation, equals the "deviation," or problem statement.
>
> *The Rational Manager,* Kepner and Tregoe (McGraw-Hill, New York, 1965).
>
> Problem-mindedness should be increased while solution-mindedness should be delayed.
>
> *Problem-Solving Discussions and Conferences,* Maier (McGraw-Hill, New York, 1963).
>
> In any problem-stating, problem-solving situation, the first responsibility of individuals involved is to understand the problem.
>
> *Synectics,* Gordon (Macmillan, New York, 1963).

For it to be useful as a management tool, we must state what is meant by *definition*. If we asked ten managers to *define* the same problem, we would probably get at least five different *definitions*. That is, the statements used to describe the problem would vary widely. To get a usable set of "definition" parameters, it is useful to refer to the scientific approach to defining. The whole process of Cause Analysis is, in fact, an application of the scientific method.

To the scientist, answering the question "why" is a lifelong goal. In the investigative process, the probing for unequivocal proof of cause requires a high level of concern. In contrast, the manager's objective is to resolve a problem, with the process of identifying real cause receiving very little attention. The scientist knows that results must be replicated on an ongoing basis. The difference lies in the degree of attention paid to the investigative process.

In the seventeenth century the English physicist Isaac Newton developed a theory for defining "matter." He identified four key criteria that all matter must have. Any complete problem definition must also include the same criteria:

1. *Identity.* If anything is to be something, it must have an identity.
2. *Location.* To be anything at all, it must exist somewhere in space. It must be, or have been, locatable.
3. *Location in Time.* To exist, "matter" must be, or have been, at some period in time.
4. *Mass.* Everything, even if it is miniscule, must have some physical dimensions.

Newton's ideas are simple and logical; they are common sense. We use an adaptation of them in our attempt to provide a rational framework for Cause Analysis. Such questions are already widely used by doctors in diagnosis:

What's wrong with you?
Where were you when you noticed the pain?
When did it start?
How frequent is the pain?
How severe is the pain?
Is it getting worse?

Any first-year student of journalism will recognize that answering the questions "who" or "what," "when," "where," and "why" provides all of the essential ingredients for an effective and objective newspaper story.

Application of Newton's theory to management, as in these other disciplines, converts these criteria to four questions: What? Where? When? Extent?

Just as good doctors ask these diagnostic questions in their offices every day, managers should ask them when they are diagnosing a business concern. The key to discovering needed information is to systematically gather these facts so that they can be used in several different ways.

THE CAUSE ANALYSIS PROCESS

In describing the process of Cause Analysis, we build a worksheet for tabulating the relevant data as we describe each step. The first data gathering should include the following description of the problem:

Identity
On what object is the defect observed?
What exactly is wrong? (defect)

Location
Where is the object with the defect observed? (geographically)
Where on the object does the defect appear?

Timing
When was the defect first observed? (clock/calendar time)
When in the life cycle of the object was the defect first observed?
In what pattern is the defect observed?

Magnitude
How much of the object is defective?
How many objects are defective?
What is the trend?

To illustrate these questions, we apply them to a specific example and then use that example to develop the complete process of Cause Analysis.

The Case of the New Terminal
An airport in a large city outside the United States opened a second passenger terminal in October several years ago. This was greeted with great sighs of relief by both airport workers and passengers. The old terminal (No. 1), although only ten years old, had not been designed to cope with the tremendous increase in passenger traffic that had occurred in the first ten years of its operation. The terminals and all support services for passengers were provided by the government airport authority. The design of the new terminal (No. 2) received awards from design councils but strong criticism from passengers. This terminal, unlike No. 1, was

designed with the capability of expansion and so was a sprawling complex of gates and buildings. Passengers complained about the long walks to gates and baggage areas.

When the new terminal was nearly ready to open, it was discovered that none of the airlines flying into that airport wanted to move from Terminal No. 1 to Terminal No. 2. This was apparently because of its starkness and inconvenient layout. The airport authority (a government body) then brought pressure on a "government airline" to move its entire operation into Terminal No. 2. Currently, all of the government airline's flights, international and national, are using Terminal No. 2. All other airlines now share Terminal 1. The largest volume of flights belong to the government airline. (Sixty percent of all air traffic in that airport is domestic flights of the government airline.) However, the government airline's international traffic represents only twenty percent of the total flight traffic, consisting primarily of flights to U.S. cities and some European and Southern charters.

A problem arose at the Terminal No. 2 customs service about a year after occupancy. The manager had determined that the number of staff grievances and complaints had increased by fifty percent in the previous six months. These ranged from "refusals to work overtime" to "complaints about the working conditions."

In an effort to resolve this problem, he checked with the immigration officers who also worked in Terminal No. 2. They had no complaints and indicated that they had observed no similar problems in Terminal No. 1. Because immigration officials moved back and forth from Terminal No. 1 to Terminal No. 2 (depending on volume), their data should have been an accurate comparison of the two. However, just to be sure, the customs manager of Terminal No. 2 called the terminal services manager in Terminal No. 1 and received confirmation of the data.

The services manager of Terminal No. 1 was surprised to hear about the problem because most of the complaining customs officers had worked with her and she considered them to be good officers. Also, the new terminal was considered by most of her staff to have better working conditions than the old and she had allocated people to Terminal No. 2 based on merit. She had, herself, received positive reports for the first few months after the transfer.

Further questioning indicated that the problem was greater on the 8 a.m.−4 p.m. shift, less on the 4 p.m.−12 p.m. shift, and almost nonexistent on the skeletal midnight shift.

The problem was surprising in that there had been no changes in supervisors, no new troublemakers added to the staff, and the heavier charter and tour business to the south during the winter had slacked off for the summer.

Based on the above information, we can begin to utilize the Cause Analysis process.

Step One.   State the Problem

Identify the object, unit, or person(s) causing the difficulty and the effects that require resolution. For example, "customs officers' grievances and informal complaints have increased by 50%." This, obviously, is undesirable and unexpected; a cause must be known before the manager can take action.

Step Two.   Describe the Problem

OBSERVED FACTS

Facts can now be assembled by asking questions in the four areas of description. Begin with a summary of critical observed facts as shown in Figure 1.1. Some very essential facts have not yet been included. A proper description must include other data if the problem is to be solved.

COMPARATIVE FACTS

In reading about the problem, one may wonder, "What about Terminal No. 1? Why the differences in shifts?" These thoughts are fundamental to a good description of the problem. Cause Analysis is a process of comparison. It is a process of creating comparative test bases. In the laboratory it is essential to create both experimental and control data. If comparisons can't be made, the key causal agent cannot be isolated. Accordingly, in Cause Analysis, the description must include the comparative data. The function of the comparative data is to isolate further the "effect" and to allow the problem solver to proceed to the cause generation stage.

Many managers react adversely to the apparently extra effort involved in generating comparative facts. However, if we extend our analogy of the scientist in the laboratory, we can see the critical need for this step. In all valid research, a scientist must provide positive proof via controlled tests that compare experimental and control studies. To be able to identify a linkage between cause and effect requires more than just a description of what happened.

In medical research new drugs are subjected to a very thorough, systematic, experimental analysis. Usually at least three groups are involved: Group A actually will be given the drug being tested. Group B will be given a placebo; this group usually is told it is being given the experimental drug. Group C usually is the control group which receives no drug or is treated in the standard treatment method. In most instances this testing is repeated many times to verify the claim of cause and effect relationship. It is this attention to the control groups and to the gathering of comparative data that provides the proof of causal relationship.

While managers may not need to be as clinically pure as medical

CAUSE ANALYSIS WORKSHEET

STEP 2. Describe Problem (good questions = good facts)	Observed Facts	Comparative Facts
What		
• On what object is the defect observed?	• Customs officers	
• What exactly is wrong (defect)?	• Increase in grievances and informal complaints (refusal to work O.T.; complaints about working conditions)	
Where		
• Where is the object with the defect observed (geographically)?	• Terminal 2	
• Where on the object does the defect appear?	• N/A	
When		
• When was the defect first observed (clock/calendar time)?	• Last 6 months (May-Oct.)	
• When in the lifecycle of the object was the defect first observed?	• Greater on shift 1 (8-4); Less on shift 2 (4-12)	
• In what pattern is the defect observed?	• N/A	
Magnitude		
• How much of the object is defective?	• Not disrupting service yet, but serious.	
• How many units/objects are defective?	• 50% increase	
• What is the trend?	• Seems to have increased since May.	

Figure 1.1   Problem description of Observed Facts.

researchers, the principle of gathering sufficient information to isolate cause is critical. The method and logical principle do not change from scientific study to management; only the depth of analysis changes.

To apply the Comparative Facts concept to our case example we have to generate a list of questions that will yield valid, precise, comparative data. Each piece of data in our first column is compared and a boundary placed on it. The net result is to provide a complete description that includes paired sets of facts that limit the problem description and provide our test base for proving a causal relationship. The key questions are:

WHAT	What object might we expect to be defective, but is not? What defect might we expect to see, but do not?
WHERE	Where else geographically could we observe the defect, but do not? Where on the object might we expect to see the defect, but do not?
WHEN	When could we have first observed the defect, but did not? (lifecycle and clock/calendar time). What might the pattern be?
MAGNITUDE	How much of the object could be defective, but is not? How many objects might we expect to be defective, but are not? What might the trend be, but is not?

Figure 1.2 demonstrates the result of applying these questions to the case example. This information clarifies the description. There is actually nothing that common sense wouldn't have suggested, but the data are now visible and we can use them for several purposes. Additionally, like all "scientific control data" they are as close, or as similar, to our experimental data as we can make them.

Step Three.   Identify Differences

As the name suggests, "comparative data" provide a basis for critically discriminating between the areas affected and those not affected. This comparison should be made to isolate the unique characteristics and features, or differences, of the problem. For example, common sense tells us that if four machines are similar and one of the four is malfunctioning, the cause of the problem will be something that is unique to that one machine. If there were nothing unique to the malfunctioning machine, then all the machines would be affected. The key to resolution lies in the ability to isolate some unique Differences causing the problem.

This concept of difference, or uniqueness, is fundamental to all problem solving. In measuring intelligence through I.Q. tests or college entrance exams, there is always a component on the ability to differentiate. The Miller Analogy Test, a fairly standard graduate school admission test, focuses on the ability to assess paired comparisons. The extension that is made from these tests is that solving problems requires that skill. The same is true in management. The ability to compare two people, two machines, or two work groups and identify the key distinction is critical for effective management.

CAUSE ANALYSIS WORKSHEET

STEP 2. Describe Problem (good questions = good facts)	Observed Facts	Comparative Facts
What		
• On what object is the defect observed?	• Customs officers	• Immigration officers
• What exactly is wrong (defect)?	• Increase in grievances and informal complaints (refused to work O.T.; complaints about working conditions)	• Absenteeism, tardiness, etc.
Where		
• Where is the object with the defect observed (geographically)?	• Terminal 2	• Terminal 1
• Where on the object does the defect appear?	• N/A	• N/A
When		
• When was the defect first observed (clock/calendar time)?	• Last 6 months (May-Oct.)	• First 6 months (Oct.-May)
• When in the lifecycle of the object was the defect first observed?	• Greater on shift 1 (8-4); Less on shift 2 (4-12)	• Shift 3 (12-8)
• In what pattern is the defect observed?	• N/A	
Magnitude		
• How much of the object is defective?	• Not disrupting service yet, but serious.	• Disrupting service; strike
• How many units/objects are defective?	• 50% increase	• Normal rate
• What is the trend?	• Seems to have increased since May.	• Single instance; decreasing

Figure 1.2   Problem description with Observed and Comparative Facts.

To further demonstrate the role of Differences, we use the following illustration:

PROBLEM PRODUCT

If we assume that A and B are comparable machines, it is reasonable to assume that both should operate in a similar manner. Since one (A) is manifesting a problem and the other (B) is not, we begin our search for cause. Basically two things can be true.

Possibility 1

The clearest, simplest explanation for this situation is that we changed something on A and not on B. Some modification, enhancement, or alteration occurred that explains the problem. In this possibility, problem solving is normally quite simple. Finding the unique event that happened to A and not to B can be relatively simple.

Possibility 2

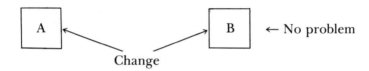

In this situation a common change was made to both A and B. The effect of that change on A, however, is different than it is on B. That leaves only one feasible explanation. Despite the fact that A and B are comparable they are not exactly the same. This means that there must be some unique feature of A that causes the different reaction. To isolate the cause and solve the problem it is critical to isolate and understand that unique feature.

This is why identifying Differences is a critical step of Cause Analysis. To implement this step the following question should be applied to every pair of facts in our definition:

Key Question.   *What is different or unique about the Observed Facts versus the Comparative Facts? The result is shown in Figure 1.3.*

Our definition of the problem is now complete. We have gathered all of the data necessary to understand the problem. As most problem solvers agree, the problem is now halfway to solution.

So far, we have used a logical questioning process to gather data, define our problem, and generate key Differences. By using specific questions, we have tried to gather only the essential, relevant facts, free from bias and independent of our experience. The questions so far have had nothing to

CAUSE ANALYSIS WORKSHEET

STEP 2. Describe Problem (good questions = good facts)	Observed Facts	Comparative Facts	Step 3. Identify Differences
What			
• On what object is the defect observed?	• Customs officers	• Immigration officers	• Customs officers always work in Terminal 2.
• What exactly is wrong (defect)?	• Increase in grievances and informal complaints (refused to work O.T.; complaints about working conditions)	• Absenteeism, tardiness, etc.	
Where			
• Where is the object with the defect observed (geographically)?	• Terminal 2	• Terminal 1	• Mostly domestic flights; lower volume of international flights • Government airline only
• Where on the object does the defect appear?	• N/A	• N/A	• Newer: different design and layout; different manager
When			
• When was the defect first observed (clock/calendar time)?	• Last 6 months (May-Oct.)	• First 6 months (Oct.-May)	• Summer season, fewer charters south
• When in the lifecycle of the object was the defect first observed?	• Greater on shift 1 (8-4); Less on shift 2 (4-12)	• Shift 3 (12-8)	
• In what pattern is the defect observed?	• N/A		
Magnitude			
• How much of the object is defective?	• Not disrupting service yet, but serious.	• Disrupting service; strike	
• How many units/objects are defective?	• 50% increase	• Normal rate	
• What is the trend?	• Seems to have increased since May.	• Single instance; decreasing	

Figure 1.3   Problem description with Differences.

do with our experience. However, experience can't be overlooked; it would be foolish to ignore it. Accordingly, the next step in the process is to draw from the "well of experience," to utilize this, along with a logical framework and our raw data, as a test mechanism.

Optional Step.   Examine and Test Experiential Cause(s)

There is no such thing as a problem without a theory of cause. Everybody has ideas about why things happen. If you are sitting with a group socially one evening, casually mention that your automobile misses and loses power as it goes up hills. An avalanche of Experiential Causes will be unleashed: "I had a car that did the same thing." "Must be the fuel pump." "Have you checked the carburetor?" "I'll bet your mixture is too thin." No one will be lacking for a cause. In such a situation it is seldom that anyone asks a question, for they are all too busy answering. When a flow of probable causes is reduced to a trickle, you might ask whether or not the fact that you drive a diesel car has any significance. This critical fact will eliminate 90% of the common causes.

The same situation occurs in management meetings. Everyone has a theory of cause. When was the last time you heard someone say, "I'm sorry, I can't speculate on a cause because I don't fully understand the problem"? We need a process step that takes this tendency into account without reducing the contribution of those involved in structured problem solving. It is very critical that we don't attempt to mold people to fit our logical process, but rather, that we relate to their experience and behavior within the context of a logical process.

Having read "The Case of the New Terminal," you may have several theories or hunches. This is the time to stop and register them. With the understanding of the definition you've gained so far, list your causes for the problem. A possible list is shown in Figure 1.4.

Let us assume that these causes represent the best list at this stage in our analysis. These causes then become our major focus. If one of them is correct, we can end the analysis and get on with the action. The critical activity now is to determine which, if any, of the three causes is correct. This leads us to test the causes.

In the early stages of Cause Analysis, we worked hard on developing a definition of our problem. This definition was created for three major purposes:

1. To clarify our understanding of the problem.
2. To provide a basis for developing causes.
3. To provide a test basis for likely causes.

It is this third purpose that we are now going to illustrate. Common sense tells us that a cause creates an effect. If the speed on a machine is increased,

---

CAUSE ANALYSIS WORKSHEET

OPTIONAL STEP. Examine and Test Experiential Causes

1. Ineffective supervision of Customs officers
2. Passenger complaints rubbing off on staff
3. Custom officers don't like the building

Figure 1.4 Experiential Causes based on "hunch" and "gut feelings."

a predictable set of effects will appear on the product of that machine. If a car is driven faster, more gas will be consumed. Because of this cause/effect relationship it is possible to increase our confidence that we have correctly identified a cause if we compare that cause against our observed effects. This is the stage in which great detectives in novels demonstrate some of their best powers of deduction. We all remember such great lines in novels as, "It couldn't have been the butler, because he is left-handed and it is obvious that the victim was killed by a right-handed, bilingual, blond-haired tennis player." As everyone gasps in astonishment at the detective's reasoning, the hero calmly and destructively tests the obvious cause against the facts.

This is exactly the process that we, as managers, must apply in resolving problems. The key is to test each cause destructively, being extremely careful not to build a case as to why it could have happened that way. In short, we must control our emotions and not fall in love with a pet theory about a cause. If a cause can survive critical, destructive testing and still explain the facts, it is a very strong cause. If, on the other hand, a cause needs assumptions, guesses, and a lot of "maybes," it is less likely to be the actual cause of the problem.

The process for testing is to take each possible cause and force-fit it to each piece of data in our definition. The key question is, "If the cause of our problem is 'ineffective supervision,' then how would it explain that we see the problem with customs officers and not immigration officers?" The answer would be that it fits because the groups had different supervisors. You would continue this testing against each set of facts until you had either found a reason for rejecting the cause, or until it completely satisfied your testing.

If we subjected our three "Experiential Causes" in "The Case of the New Terminal" to this test, we would find the following:

Cause No. 1	Does Not Explain
Ineffective supervision of customs officers.	Complaints began six months before problem was recognized. If supervision had been ineffective, complaints would have started earlier.
	No changes had been made in supervisors or method of supervision since moving into Terminal No. 2 in October.
	Why hadn't the customs officers, who were the "best," specifically complained about ineffective supervision instead of overtime and poor working conditions?

	Cause No. 2
Passenger complaints rubbing off on staff.	Why customs and not immigration? Why grievances about overtime? Why certain shifts only?

	Cause No. 3
Customs officers didn't like the building.	Why customs and not immigration officers? Why complain about overtime? Why after six months of occupancy? Should have been immediate. Why only two shifts?

It seems that our first attempt at finding the cause has left us with some question marks. It hasn't given us a cause on which we would be willing to take action. If this is the case, we need to further develop possible causes if we are going to correct the problem and remove those effects.

Step Four.   List Changes

Since our first attempt at developing causes was very much tied to our experience, it is now useful to utilize the data we have gathered.

Again, we must refer to Isaac Newton and borrow some of his principles. One of his laws of motion said something to the effect that "a body in motion tends to continue moving in the same direction, unless acted upon by an outside force." In Cause Analysis, this principle is critical. If something is operating at a certain standard (e.g., a machine is producing 500 units per hour), unless something causes a change in performance, the operation can be expected to continue at that standard. This concept of change is shown in Figure 1.5.

Common sense tells us that somehow, somewhere, something changed in or around the point at which the divergence becomes visible. The thesis is "cause = change." We are suggesting that the cause of the problem can often, if not always, be found in a Change.

Using this simple change/cause theory, we can develop some theories of cause by listing key Changes. Listing all Changes would be thorough and perhaps useful, but it is unrealistic. Too many things change within an environment every day. What we need to do is to isolate and list only relevant Changes. For our purposes the definition of "relevant" is "something that relates to the observed facts." We went to a lot of trouble to identify Differences which we now use to identify relevant changes. The process is to take each Difference in turn and list any Changes identified with that feature. Figure 1.6 reflects the result of applying the search for Changes to our list of differences. To develop these Changes we apply the following key question:

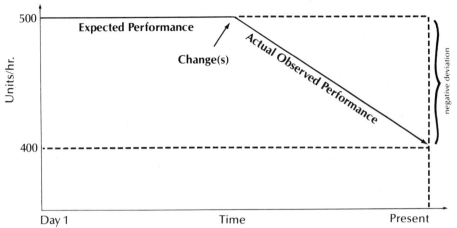

Figure 1.5 Graphic representation of the concept of change. Notice that without a change there will be no deviation.

CAUSE ANALYSIS WORKSHEET

STEP 3. Identify Differences	STEP 4. List Changes	STEP 5. & 6. Generate Likely Causes and Test
• Customs officers always work in Terminal 2.	• No change since Oct. last year	
• Mostly domestic flights; lower volume of international flights	• Decreased work load in Terminal 2.	
• Government airline only	• Servicing one airline only	
• New or different design and layout	• Working environment different	
• Different manager	• No change	
• Summer season; fewer charters south	• Further reduction in work load (decreased international flights)	

Figure 1.6 Listing of changes from each Difference.

Key Question.   *What has changed in, about, or around these Differences? (Date the Changes.)*

Step Five.   Generate Likely Causes

These Changes can now be utilized to help us develop likely causes. We now begin to utilize our experience with these new data and ask the same key cause question we asked earlier:

Key Question.   *How could this Change alone or in combination with a Difference have caused this problem?*

The key Change is decreased workload. This Change should be explored for potential causes. Since the work of customs clearance had been split between two terminals, perhaps there wasn't enough work to keep people busy. Terminal No. 2 had less traffic and the work was erratic. Infrequent international flights caused irregular work.

Step Six.   Test Most Likely Cause

If we now apply our testing question, as we did in testing Experiential Causes, we can see if this cause fits the facts of the case.

Key Question.   *How does this cause explain the Observed versus the Comparative Facts?*

As shown in Figure 1.7, this cause, although not perfect, seems to fit. It explains "customs versus immigration" because immigration officers moved from terminal to terminal, based on volume. It explains Terminal No. 2 versus Terminal No. 1 because there were fewer flights and more no-work periods between flights. It explains why the problem erupted in the last six months, and not before, because the package tour business to the south which was filling the gap was then in its "down" period. The only question remaining is the issue of "Why not Shift No. 3 $(12-8)$?"

Step Seven.   Verify Most Likely Cause

Because this cause seemed the most probable, the manager went out to check this theory with the staff. First he went to the Shift No. 3 supervisor, explained his analysis to date, and asked if there were any missing data to clarify the question (see Figure 1.8).

The supervisor immediately responded that everyone on Shift No. 3

CAUSE ANALYSIS WORKSHEET

STEP 3. Identify Differences	STEP 4. List Changes	STEP 5. & 6. Generate Likely Causes and Test
• Customs officers always work in Terminal 2.	• No change since Oct. last year	• Not enough work to keep Customs people busy. (Does not explain: Why isn't Shift 3 (12-8) affected?)
• Mostly domestic flights; lower volume of international flights	• Decreased work load in Terminal 2.	
• Government airline only	• Servicing one airline only	
• New or different design and layout	• Working environment different	
• Different manager	• No change	
• Summer season; fewer charters south	• Further reduction in work load (decreased international flights)	

Figure 1.7 Statement of Likely Causes and testing.

CAUSE ANALYSIS WORKSHEET

STEP 7. Verify Most Likely Cause

• Not enough work (talk with staff to get any missing data, re: Shift 3)

Figure 1.8 The verification step is the final process step in Standard Cause Analysis. Now it is time to go check it out.

expected long periods of down time. There were always fewer flights midnight to 8 a.m. and, in most cases, his skeletal crew chose this shift so that they could have the free time. Two of them were finishing university degrees during the day and did a lot of reading and assignments during this shift. They wouldn't trade Shift 3 in Terminal No. 2 for anything.

Further meetings with the staff confirmed that the major cause of the problem lay in the variable workload of the new terminal. When a wide-bodied jet arrived all persons were busy for an hour. There were frequent intervals of 1 or 2 hours, however, when only a minimal amount of customs clearance were required. If a flight was delayed to near the end of a shift the effect was more severe. By looking logically at the facts, the manager was able to come to a rational conclusion, to check it out, and plan some proper corrective action, rather than simply react to the situation.

If the manager had reacted to the emotions of the situation and had begun to take actions to resolve the symptoms, he could have made the situation even worse. If he had changed the supervisor or tried to modify the working conditions, he would have been wasting time and money.

The Cause Analysis framework provides a method for analyzing information to find the cause of a problem. The steps are labels attached to normal managerial common sense. Normally any analyzed data is assessed, even if in a superficial review. What may be different in the framework is a logical progression. The facts are only as important as the ability to use and build upon them.

One by-product of structured analysis is to change the rules of the "Blame Ball" game. In many organizations the key role of emotional, rather than logical, cause analysis is to be able to attach blame. The "Blame Ball" gets batted around much the same as a ball in a baseball game and managers get a distinct message that "three strikes and you're out." Claims of "foul ball" are not necessarily accepted. If somehow organizations could transfer all the energy exerted in batting the "Blame Ball" to logical Cause Analysis, there would be a tremendous increase in problem solving.

A flowchart (Figure 1.9) and worksheet (Figure 1.10) are included here for further reference. A Cause Analysis case study, *Riverside,* provides an opportunity for practice. A sample resolution is located in the Appendix. Several real applications of Cause Analysis follow the case study.

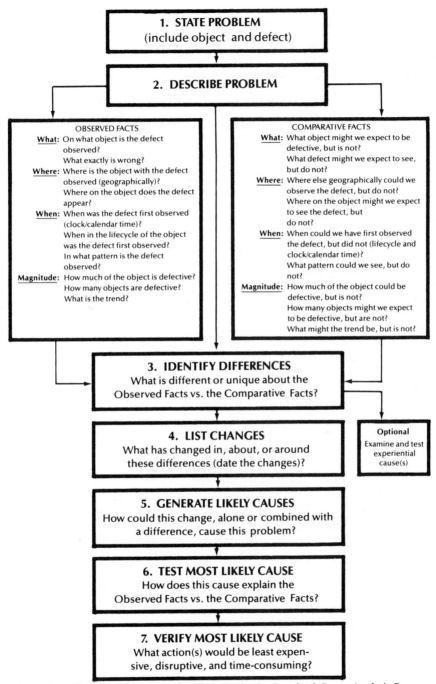

1. STATE PROBLEM
(include object and defect)

2. DESCRIBE PROBLEM

OBSERVED FACTS

<u>What</u>: On what object is the defect observed?
What exactly is wrong?

<u>Where</u>: Where is the object with the defect observed (geographically)?
Where on the object does the defect appear?

<u>When</u>: When was the defect first observed (clock/calendar time)?
When in the lifecycle of the object was the defect first observed?
In what pattern is the defect observed?

<u>Magnitude</u>: How much of the object is defective?
How many objects are defective?
What is the trend?

COMPARATIVE FACTS

<u>What</u>: What object might we expect to be defective, but is not?
What defect might we expect to see, but do not?

<u>Where</u>: Where else geographically could we observe the defect, but do not?
Where on the object might we expect to see the defect, but do not?

<u>When</u>: When could we have first observed the defect, but did not (lifecycle and clock/calendar time)?
What pattern could we see, but do not?

<u>Magnitude</u>: How much of the object could be defective, but is not?
How many objects might we expect to be defective, but are not?
What might the trend be, but is not?

3. IDENTIFY DIFFERENCES
What is different or unique about the
Observed Facts vs. the Comparative Facts?

4. LIST CHANGES
What has changed in, about, or around
these differences (date the changes)?

Optional
Examine and test experiential cause(s)

5. GENERATE LIKELY CAUSES
How could this change, alone or combined with
a difference, cause this problem?

6. TEST MOST LIKELY CAUSE
How does this cause explain the
Observed Facts vs. the Comparative Facts?

7. VERIFY MOST LIKELY CAUSE
What action(s) would be least expensive, disruptive, and time-consuming?

Figure 1.9 Flowchart demonstrating the steps in the Standard Cause Analysis Process.

CAUSE ANALYSIS WORKSHEET

STEP 1. State Problem (include object and defect)

STEP 2. Describe Problem (good questions = good facts)	Observed Facts	Comparative Facts
What • On what object is the defect observed? • What exactly is wrong (defect)? **Where** • Where is the object with the defect observed (geographically)? • Where on the object does the defect appear? **When** • When was defect first observed (clock/calendar time)? • When in the lifetime of the object was the defect first observed? • In what pattern is the defect observed? **Magnitude** • How much of the object is defective? • How many objects are defective? • What is the trend?		

OPTIONAL STEP. Examine and Test Experiential Causes

Figure 1.10 Worksheet outlining the steps

STEP 3. Identify Differences	STEP 4. List Changes	STEP 5. and 6. Generate Likely Causes and Test

STEP 7. Verify Most Likely Cause

in the Standard Cause Analysis Process.

RIVERSIDE

General Statement

The Riverside Maintenance Station, located at Andersonville, is responsible for the repair and upkeep of interstate and state highways in District Four of the State Highway System. The Riverside Station (RMS) has important responsibility for heavily traveled traffic routes. The district includes the large population center at Andersonville and the state capitol of Haven and contains a major east-west trucking route as well. The territory encompasses 225 miles of four- to six-lane highways (see Figure 1.11). The jurisdiction of the RMS also includes the non-toll bridge at Greenland, but excludes the two toll bridges in the district at Andersonville and River City which are under the control of a separate bridge unit within the State Department of Transportation.

The responsibilities of the RMS have been the same since 1973 except that the Salmon Highway above the Greenland Bridge was upgraded from a two-lane road with no center dividers to a major thoroughfare last April and the extension of Deer Highway from River City to Pepperly was completed and opened about two and a half years ago. This construction and upgrading work was performed by private contractors. There has been no major new road construction in the state since, largely because of a state government moratorium on construction of new highways due to the gasoline shortages.

The working staff of the RMS is composed of forty experienced and apprenticed highway workers. During the year, workers are allocated either to minor resurfacing operations or to repairing existing road surfaces, guardrails, road shoulders, and maintaining plant life along the highways. (Sample road work reports are shown in Figure 1.12.) The RMS obtains asphalt, concrete, gravel, and all other materials directly from suppliers and has all its own equipment to maintain and repair the roads.

All major upgrading and road construction as well as major resurfacing jobs are contracted out to private firms. These projects are determined on a need basis. Several different contractors have been used throughout the years, some more successfully than others. Amico Construction did a good job with the construction of the Deer Highway Extension, the only major highway in the district requiring a land fill operation prior to actual road construction, but the paving job was rough and necessitated a resurfacing job by the Danko Company last summer.

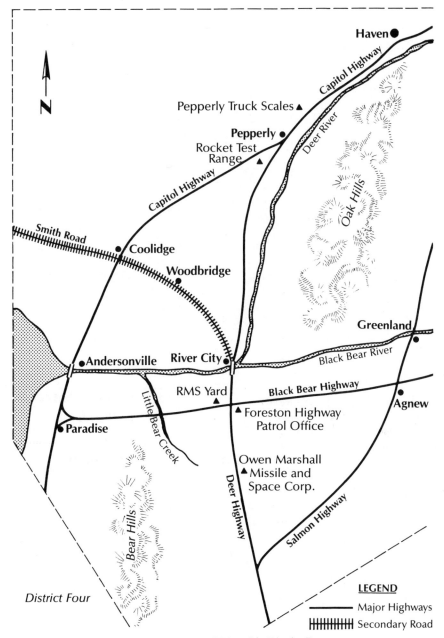

Figure 1.11 Map of Riverside District Four.

Date	Crew	Assigned to:	Comments
1	3	Smith : plants	
2	3	"	
3	3	"	
4	1	Smith / Capitol	
5	2	plants stand-by	weekend
6	2	"	weekend
7	4	Capitol - plants	windy
8	5	" - guardrails	
9	6	Deer - plants	
10	6	"	
11	6	"	
12	7	stand-by	weekend
13	7	"	"
14	8	Black Bear - plants	
15	8	" "	light rain
16	9	Salmon - plants	"
17	9	" "	"
18	10	yard	gale warnings - heavy rain
19	1	stand-by	weekend
20	1	"	"
21	2	Salmon - guardrails	light rain
22	2	" "	rain
23	4	" - fences	thunderstorm
24	4	stand-by	holiday
25	4	"	"
26	4	stand-by	weekend
27	5	"	"
28	5	Salmon - fences	heavy rain
29	5	" "	light rain
30		" - plants	winds
31			

Figure 1.12   Road work reports for the Riverside District.

Date	Crew	Assigned to:	Comments
1	6	Black Bear -rails	light rain
2	7	" -fences	heavy "
3	8	stand-by	weekend
4	8	"	"
5	9	Capitol - guardrails	light rain
6	10	" -fences	clear
7	1	"	"
8	2	yard	heavy rain
9	2	"	"
10	3	stand-by	weekend
11	3	"	"
12	4	Capitol - fences	light rain
13	5	Salmon - fences	"
14	5	" "	light rain
15	6	" - line painting	
16	7	Black Bear - lines	
17	8,9,10,1 110 O.T.	Deer Ext. - surface	
18	8,9,10,1 120 O.T.	" "	light rain
19	2,3,4,5 80 O.T.	" "	rain
20	2,3,4,5 80 O.T.	" "	light rain
21	6	" "	"
22	6	" "	winds / rain
23	6	" "	" "
24	7	stand-by	weekend
25	7	"	"
26	7	"	holiday
27	8	Deer Ext. - surface	
28	8	" "	rain
29	8	" "	"
30	8	" "	"
31	9	stand-by	holiday

(O.T.= overtime hours)

Figure 1.12   Continued.

Date	Crew	Assigned to:	Comments
1	10	stand-by	weekend
2	10	"	holiday
3	1	yard	heavy rain
4	2	Capitol – on ramp flooding	heavy rain
5	3	Salmon – flooding	"
6	4	Deer Ext. – surface	
7	4,5/40 O.T.	" "	weekend
8	6,4/40 O.T.	" "	"
9	7	" "	heavy rain
10	8	" "	winds – "
11	9	" "	light rain
12	10	" "	"
13	1	" "	"
14	2	stand-by	weekend
15	2	"	"
16	2	Deer Ext. – surface	"
17	3	" "	light rain
18	4	" "	heavy rain
19	5	" "	"
20	6	" "	"
21	7	stand-by	weekend
22	7	"	"
23	8	Deer Ext. – surface	rains
24	9	" "	heavy rains
25	10	" "	"
26	1	" "	winds – rains
27	2	" "	"
28	3	stand-by	weekend
29	3	"	"
30	4	Deer Ext. – surface	rain
31	5	" "	"

(O.T. = overtime hours)

Figure 1.12 Continued.

Date	Crew	Assigned to:	Comments
1	6	Black Bear - plants	
2	7	Capitol - plants	light rain
3	8	Smith - fences	heavy rain
4	9	stand-by	weekend
5	9	"	"
6	10	yard	heavy storms
7	1	⃰	" rains
8	2	Smith - fences	rain
9	3	Salmon & Deer - guardrails	
10	4,5/48 O.T.	Deer Ext. - surface	
11	4,5,6/80 O.T.	" "	weekend
12	4,5,6,7/120 O.T.	" "	weekend
13	8	" "	winds
14	8	" "	rain
15			
16			
17			
18			
19			
20			
21			
22			
23			
24			
25			
26			
27			
28			
29			
30			
31			

(O.T. = overtime hours)

Figure 1.12 Continued.

Because of the long drought, which lasted from early 1979 until mid-November of last year, a separate vendor, Capitol Engineers, Inc., also resurfaced a section of Salmon Highway from Agnew to Greenland in December 1979. All resurfacing and most major construction is typically done only in the summer months as rainy weather prohibits such work. Usually some layoffs occur at RMS in the winter months, as repair work alone does not justify a full staff.

Because of consistently low bids and reliable performance, the Danko Company is frequently chosen as a vendor. They completed the resurfacing of Deer Highway from Pepperly to the southern border of District 4, and Capitol Highway between Andersonville and Pepperly, although they did have a difficult time finishing the jobs on schedule last summer. Just before starting the season, a severe strike hit their materials supplier. In order to continue work, they were forced to obtain materials from a different, nonunion supplier. As the company had a policy of using only union suppliers, this caused some unhappiness and complaining among the crew members. The strike was so long and bitter that it eventually bankrupted the materials firm. People lost their jobs and feelings ran high in the small towns where many of them lived.

Last June, the Danko Company hired several new workers to comply with an affirmative action order. This action created serious conflicts for some of the regulars, none of whom had ever worked with women on the road crew before. A few men threatened to quit on the spot, but the foreman convinced them to give it a try and it seems to be working out. Today most of the major construction and contracting firms, including Amico and Capitol Engineers, Inc., employ women on their crews.

In general, things have gone pretty well over the last few years throughout District Four. Despite higher trafffic throughout the District, the number of accidents due to road conditions didn't increase through the end of 1980. There are plans to correct the three historically worst traffic accident spots this summer: the end of the archaic two-lane bridge at Greenland, the toll plaza at Andersonville, and the interchange at Paradise. An earthquake measuring 4.3 on the Richter scale just after Christmas and centered just above Pepperly caused no accidents and no visible damage to the highway system, but neighboring districts haven't been so trouble free. Many of them have experienced severe road sinking or buckling because the water table dropped during the drought. Also, there are increased safety problems due to increased traffic load on highways in many areas.

The Situation: February 15, 1981

Recently, however, things haven't been so smooth in District Four. For one thing, last September demonstrators managed to block traffic on Deer Highway by the rocket testing range as they protested the army's increased testing on a newly developed rocket motor which could be used for nuclear weapons. There was quite a commotion and the demonstrators managed for three whole days to block the normally heavy traffic from River City to Pepperly, including military convoys and missile carriers. The demonstration caused several accidents which considerably damaged guardrails. The RMS crews have repaired these as time has allowed. The demonstrators were cleared away by the police and, though they still picket the testing range occasionally, have been unable to interrupt the Monday through Friday schedule of testing. Since this same group of protestors is suspected of blowing up several utility towers in the state a few years ago, police are keeping a close eye on the situation.

The RMS work crews, usually partially laid off at this time, have been kept at full strength for the guardrail repairs necessitated by the earlier accidents. This is actually quite lucky as, beginning in mid-December, truckers and the highway patrol began complaining about the number of potholes on Deer Highway between River City and Pepperly. Repairs have been made—as weather allowed—but holes continue to appear. The crews have therefore been working overtime, rather than being laid off. The budget is a shambles, and last week word came down that the district was being sued for damages in two accidents caused by negligent maintenance on Deer Highway.

Certainly these potholes could have caused an accident. One pothole— the biggest one reported—measured over thirty-six inches across and over sixteen inches down. Some stretches of the Deer Highway Extension have reported up to twenty potholes per mile. At times, when repairs could not be made right away, traffic has been limited to the left lanes of the highway. Complaints from users of the highway have been many and loud; the construction delays have been as long as two hours in duration.

To make things worse, even after the potholes reported in December were filled and repaired, fresh potholes have appeared in the same places. Not only is the highway rough from repair operations but new holes frequently appear in other stretches of the same road. New holes were reported on and off during January all along this stretch of Deer Highway and a new rash of holes was just reported last week.

The situation has reached a critical level with these latest test reports. Along with the two lawsuits, District Four has to contend with letters of complaint written to the county by several large trucking firms. The local head of the highway patrol has called several county commissioners about the problem. The military has also complained loudly through the local commander and the U.S. Representative for the district. The work crew is still on overtime; it will be next week before repairs are completed and even then the road surface will be very rough.

RMS is considering a legal action against the Danko Company, which did the resurfacing last summer; that could result in losing the service of a previously reliable contractor. Without knowing the cause of the problem it is difficult to decide what action to take.

Crew members of the Riverside Maintenance Station have begun arguing about the cause of the potholes. They are tired of working on the same road and things are definitely getting worse. The manager of RMS has requested input from the lead crew foreman.

MEMORANDUM

To:

From: Lead Crew Foreman

After checking with the various crew members, I am really not much further along than when we spoke last week.

Pete feels strongly that Danko is responsible, but truthfully, his bias is against the women crew members. He may be right—maybe girls can't do this kind of road work. Another thought on that line is that because last summer was the first time the Danko crew worked with girls, *they* may have been distracted.

I also discussed the problem with Jim Samuels, and he feels strongly that these holes must be directly related to the testing going on at the rocket testing range. He thinks the place to start is with monitoring the area for vibrations caused by motor testing and then simulating the effect of similar vibrations on a mock-up road or road surface. That could take a long time and be fairly costly—but if the government is to blame, so what!! All those demonstrations have not managed to halt motor tests, so how could we? Still we might get some compensation from the Feds for damages.

A similar theory that emerged from a discussion with a couple of the second crew apprentices is that the earthquake last December did some subsurface damage, undermining the foundation. That doesn't make much sense to me though because we haven't seen any damage at the area hardest hit—above Pepperly on the Capitol Highway. I did pull the road work reports for the past few months and have attached a copy for your review. Maybe if we go over them together we can find some correlation between these theories.

What is the cause of this problem?

What action would you recommend?

AUTOMATIC SHOWER PROBLEM

A small plant that manufactures particle board from waste corrugated medium (cardboard boxes) had a serious concern. The problem occurred repeatedly over a period of several months following the installation of an automatic control system. It went unsolved until a group of managers trained in Cause Analysis tackled the problem.

The company manufactures a product from waste products. It repulps the waste products and puts them into a solution with approximately twenty percent solids and eighty percent water. It pumps this solution through a series of pipes from a smaller to a larger diameter from the basement of the pulping operation to the top floor where the forming machine is located.

The pulping solution is then pumped into a machine with a screening device that permits the particles to join together, by allowing the water to drain through leaving just the particles. This forming device is carried on a conveyor system that moves it from one point of consistency to points of greater and greater consistency (i.e., drier and drier points) until finally it reaches a point where it can safely be moved onto another conveyor system that removes additional water. Eventually the product goes through a series of dryers where it becomes a solid.

The difficulty appeared at the first conveyor system. As the pulp was pumped onto the system, much of the water drained off; a shower arrangement over the system could add more water if the pulp was too dry. Until recently, this had been done by an employee who grabbed handfuls of pulp to determine by touch whether more water was needed. A number of months previous to the problem's occurrence, an automatic control system had been placed on the equipment. It provided for the constant measurement of the consistency of the pulp and therefore the constant adding or taking away of water on the first conveyor system. The problem statement indicated that "while on automatic control, the shower adds water when it does not need water or tries to take away water when it does." Occasionally, the shower worked properly.

This problem was very frustrating for the company. The equipment was expensive and allowed the company to eliminate several jobs, thus contributing to a low morale problem. "I told you so" was frequently heard. The company's engineering group and the vendor almost rebuilt the

43

system in an attempt to find and correct the cause. Meanwhile, the operators would routinely switch the device from the automatic to the manual position and manipulate it as before (but with greater difficulties).

A group of managers decided to solve this problem using the Cause Analysis process. While describing the problem, they focused on the time pattern. Until then, the word "periodic" had been used to describe the pattern. The managers, using the automatic control system daily recorder charts, reviewed the last several months, looking for the exact pattern of the problem. They learned that on some shifts the equipment operated properly on automatic and on other shifts it did not. It worked for several hours, at some points operating properly, at others stopping after just a few minutes. But it always operated properly on manual.

The group of managers described the pattern point-by-point, beginning with the second week of installation. The equipment had started working at 1:00 a.m. on the 14th and gone from 1:00 to 2:45 a.m. with no problems. At 2:45 a.m. it had begun to malfunction, and continued to do so from 2:45 to about 4:00 a.m. at which point the foreman had switched the system to manual. It had stayed on manual for the remainder of that shift and for four hours of the next shift. At 11:00 a.m. the next day it had been switched back to automatic and ran properly. In the interim, some adjustments had been made.

The team of managers continued to describe the pattern of the problem, using the recorder charts—the actual information. It became apparent that there must have been something unusual done at the times when the problem occurred compared to the points in time when it did not. What were the Differences? Until that time, they had been unable to discover the Differences because of the vague problem description, "periodic" and not "constant."

Now with some solid information they could look at it more specifically. What had occurred on that second day from 1:00 a.m. until 2:45 a.m. and so forth? After a while they noticed that they had been running different weights, or grades, of paper during that time. It was apparent that the problem occurred more frequently with heavier grade products than with lighter ones. The grade changes in the order processing log were compared to the pattern of the problem. There was almost a perfect correlation between the problem's occurrence and the use of the heaviest grades of paper.

The initial installation of the system had included a metering device that constantly monitored the consistency of the pulp passing through the pipe. The device was located in a length of pipe in the basement. The system worked by determining the coefficient of friction and computing the drag ratio; that is, it was the "rudder" beneath the boat. As the product was pumped past this particular "rudder," the drag created on its surface would determine the actual consistency at that point. The device would signal the showers upstairs and eventually the valves would open or close and water be added to or removed from the pulp.

The cause of the problem was that the pipe that housed the "rudder" was 12 feet shorter than the design specification. This created a velocity much greater than the "rudder" could accurately measure. The combined effect of the higher velocity and the heavier grades of pulp on the meter caused the valves to overreact which caused the problem.

Experience shows that the cause of many problems can be found through a close examination of the time pattern. In this case, the *actual* pattern of facts quickly led to the discovery of the cause of the problem.

BOILER SYSTEM MALFUNCTION

A large smelting operation experienced a critical problem with an automatic boiler feed system. A group of technicians solved the problem using Cause Analysis.

The problem had plagued the company for six months. Loss of production time aside, the boiler was also failing to provide hot water for the workers' showers. Since the outside temperature had reached fifteen below zero, this problem had become a major issue. The company and the manufacturer of the boiler had attempted to solve the problem by replacing numerous parts, readjusting time setting, etc.—all to no avail.

The boiler was located in the east end of the plant compound. It operated through a series of automatic control devices such as pumps, valves, and gauges. The controls monitored the amount of fuel fed into the boiler—to get maximum use from the boiler during peak periods and save fuel during slow periods. This was all done automatically.

The problem was that the boiler would not reignite while on automatic control. It was first reported six months before the technicians tackled it; there seemed to be no set pattern. To establish comparative data, the technicians compared it with another, standard model boiler that was smaller and manually operated; its valves were opened and closed at a set time, by hand. In reviewing the comparative facts, the technicians saw that the problem clearly had not occurred prior to six months before.

The specific information in the *"WHEN" dimension* of Cause Analysis is almost always critical to the solution of the problem. Considering this, the group of technicians reexamined the facts. The boiler had an automatic monitoring device on it (a twenty-four-hour recorder). The technicians reviewed the daily charts from the last six months and discovered that the problem did have a precise pattern. The pattern was that as the boiler finished a six-hour load representing its peak, it went into a two-and-one-half-hour holding state during which time it burned no fuel and maintained its temperature. At the end of the holding period, the boiler was supposed to re-ignite, a valve would open automatically and the boiler would evacuate all gases. The exhaust valves were then to close and a small amount of gas would be monitored into the boiler by a pilot valve. An electric ignition spark then would turn on and stay on until the gas ignited at which point the spark would turn off. The gas would burn for a few seconds, then another valve open and let more gas into the system. Other valves were supposed to open sequentially until they were all open. The boiler temperature was regulated by opening and closing valves.

The daily charts indicated that the problem's occurrence coincided with the times when the electric spark was supposed to turn on. Ignition could not be confirmed because the inspection porthole was dirty; the technicians could not see inside the boiler. They analyzed this new-found information by finding differnces between conditions when the problem occurred and those when it did not. They discovered that the Differences, or unique characteristics, were (1) the electric spark itself, (2) the duration of the electric spark, and (3) the opening and closing of the initial valve. Aside from that, conditions were the same.

They analyzed to find changes by asking, "What has changed about the opening and closing of the valve?" and "What has changed in and around the electric spark?" Nothing could be confirmed visually due to the dirty porthole. Finally they reasoned that the most likely cause was the electric spark is not staying on long enough to ignite the gas. If that was so, why did the problem occur when it did? The technicians verified the cause by removing the control from the electric spark so that they could manually control it. The boiler then ignited perfectly.

As it turned out, the cause of the problem was that the electric spark was not staying on long enough to ignite the gas during cold weather. The spark was supposed to stay on until either ignition had occurred or four seconds had elapsed. Ignition was supposed to be reflected in a mirror inside the boiler. The mirror was supposed to reflect the light of the flame, which would extinguish the spark and begin the opening of the valves but the mirror was as dirty as the porthole. What actually happened was that when the gas came in, the spark would come on, and, since the dirty porthole and mirror did not reflect ignition, it would automatically turn off after four seconds. Unfortunately, four seconds was not enough time during cold weather.

The point to be learned from this situation is that the information that most often solves a problem is in the "WHEN" dimension. The questions "When in the lifecycle?" and "What is the time pattern?" provide the key information.

SCREWDRIVER MACHINE OVERRIDE

A difficult problem existed in a company that made electrical switching gear. The company manufactured and assembled various components.

The problem occurred on one of the automatic screwdriver machines that are used to assemble three components into a single component. These machines had been a problem for a number of years and the manufacturer had routinely come in and adjusted them. The problem was a recurring one and was quite a headache for the operators, maintenance people, and management.

In attempting to solve this problem, a group of the company's maintenance technicians trained in Cause Analysis described the problem as: "The automatic screwdriver machine does not work properly." Technically, this means that when a screw was inserted into the components and the screwdriver attempted to set the screw automatically it occasionally burred the screw (i.e., overrode the slotted head and so made it unusable). Consequently, the machine had to be stopped, and the screw removed by hand and discarded. The operator then had to start all over. It was readily apparent that the screwheads were being marred by the screwdriver tip, but what was the cause of the screwdriver tip's overriding the screwhead?

A closer examination showed that the screws were not being properly inserted into the component and therefore were already misaligned when the screwdriver tip descended to screw them into place. The automatic screwdriver would simply override them and mar the top of the screwhead. But what caused the misalignment? The original problem statement was "The automatic screwdriver machine does not work properly." This was narrowed down to a more specific problem statement that said "The automatic screwdriver machine is not inserting the screws properly." The technicians' attempt to describe the problem was frustrating because the exact timing of the problem was lost; no one could remember when these problems had first started.

The team decided to concentrate on "when in the lifecycle" it had occurred. It was described as happening "just as the screwdriver attempts to turn the screw." The team next focused on the pattern of the problem. Their information was vague, but the pattern appeared to be sporadic or intermittent. In this instance, it was necessary for the technicians to create their own information. They had the operators start the machine and operate it for approximately one hour while they observed, looking for "when in the lifecycle" and "time pattern." They made a grid and counted the screws as they were inserted. There were ten positions at which the screws were to be inserted and tightened down. The automatic screw machine followed the same pattern with each one since the automatic screw machine screwdriver was mounted on a stylus which followed prescribed pattern.

The operator took the three components, put them together in a "sandwich" form, placed them on the board, and locked them down. The automatic screwdriver machine moved to the first position and descended. The operator then pulled a trigger and it injected a screw and tightened it down; then it moved to position two, three, and so forth, with the operator merely touching the trigger at each screw position. The automatic screw-driver followed the same route on all components. Once the circuit was completed, the operator would release the handle and a spring would move the automatic screwdriver out of the way. The component was removed and a new one put in its place before the procedure was repeated.

Over a period of one hour, the team noticed some interesting facts. First of all, they discovered that there was a very exact pattern to the problem; it seemed to occur most often in positions one, four, five, and ten. It occurred in other positions occasionally, but most often in these four. What was different about these positions compared to the others? A closer examina-tion showed that (1) number one position was the starting position, (2) four and five were two of the recessed positions, and (3) the number ten position was the last one.

Further analysis disclosed that these positions were the points where the most stress was placed on the automatic screw machine. At the first position, the operator pulled the head into position with a jerk to overcome the spring action and then pulled down to insert the screw. The screwhead followed the stylus forward to the second and third positions, and the operator then pushed downward to insert screws in the recessed positions (four, five, six, and seven). The machine then came back and easily went to positions eight and nine, before being pushed to the rear to position ten. When the machine was finished with all ten positions, the operator released the handle and a spring load pulled the screwdriver head approximately twelve to fifteen inches back to the original starting position.

The cause turned out to be the excess wear of the stylus table at these positions. Naturally, over a period of time this usage had worn the grooves in the table down a bit. At the points where there was greater exertion, there was also greater wear. Therefore, the extra wear caused misalign-ment causing the screwdriver head to occasionally override and mar the tops of the screws.

In summary, the team used Cause Analysis to create precise information about the problem. They knew which facts were needed; the next step was to create information through observation. A second key factor was the need to respecify the problem statement to a lower level on the cause/effect chain. "Automatic screwdriver doesn't work" was converted to "Misalignment of screwdriver and insertion of screws."

MISLABELED CHEMICALS

In a plant that manufactures very complicated electronic test equipment, one particular manufacturer had literally sunk all of their eggs in one basket. They developed a particular piece of portable test equipment which sold for $22,000 and for which the demand was estimated to be over 10,000 units worldwide.

Market acceptance was fantastic, beyond the manufacturer's greatest expectations, and it was estimated that, because of the sophisticated nature of the product, it would take competitors about two and a half years to develop and market anything similar. Manufacturing was capable of producing ten units per day and was working six days per week. Everything looked rosy; orders were running six months ahead of production and growing. Then all hell broke loose!

At first the reports of field failures began to trickle in. Then they rose steadily to an astonishing 60%. Various consulting engineering firms were called in on six different occasions. The problem apparently fed on itself because of the compactness of the product. A unit would come in from the field to be fixed; it would be repaired and returned to the field—only to fail for a different reason in another few weeks.

Exactly one-half of the production line's time was spent on repair, so that production dropped to five units per day. There seemed to be no single failure that predominated. It was felt, however, that so many errors on the production floor warranted calling in a consultant in Cause Analysis.

A group of twelve assemblers was instructed in the process of Cause Analysis and told to select a particular problem that interested them and solve it by using this process. One particular problem selected was a small one. It seemed that fuse holders, 4¢ parts, were breaking on the line. They snapped in place in a square hole cut for just that purpose in the back of the equipment. The fuse holders were held in place by four tabs molded into the holder. The fuses were placed in the rear of the equipment by simply "snapping" them into place. The fuse holders also had two heavy leads to which the main power supply wires were connected by solder. Later on the fuses themselves were placed in a fuse housing, so it was a simple matter of the power coming from its source into the lead through the fuses, then out through the other leads to the internal parts.

What had been noticed by one operator at final test was that sometimes a unit came through that had one or more of the tabs on the side of the fuse housing broken off. Fixing it was a simple matter of removing the old housing and snapping in a new one. She also had to cut the main power wires, trim them, and resolder the leads. It was a simple operation that took only a few minutes. Finding out why some of the fuse housing tabs were broken could not be considered a "big" fix because of the small cost of the part and the short time required to fix it. Nevertheless, every problem has a cause and she, with the help of her group and instructor, went after it.

The cause simply couldn't be found though. The process kept leading to the conclusion that operator error was at fault. But operators were observed and no error could be detected. It was, after all, such a simple operation:

1. Snap in the fuse housing.
2. Solder two leads.

   3. Clean the solder joints.

   4. Send the unit on its way.

How, given such a simple operation, could there be an operator error? For a week the fuse housings were checked against the specs, tested in the lab, the operator was observed, etc.,—nothing.

After a week, when everyone had just about given up, they could think of just one more way to test for operator error. They brought ten fuse housings into the classroom and swabbed one with the cleaning solution. The tabs fell off! They brushed another one with the solution and the tabs fell off again! How could that be? The solder joints were cleaned with alcohol, which is not corrosive to plastic. The answer, of course, was obvious: though the cleaning solution label said alcohol, it actually contained something else. They all stared at one another in stunned silence . . . there was no chemical control on the line, and never had been since the production line had started. If that were true, then every time a connection was cleaned the corrosive solution would splatter randomly on all sorts of parts and could cause a variety of field failures!

All chemicals were withdrawn from the line. It was determined that all bottles used to contain alcohol did, in fact, contain it—all, that is, except two, and they contained a highly corrosive liquid.

Since that time field failures have steadily declined to a ten percent level.

CAUSE ANALYSIS VARIATIONS

In the beginning of the chapter on Cause Analysis we explored the process for identifying cause in relatively straightforward cause/effect situations. The cause/effect relationship was traceable, clear, and verifiable. In many instances, however, the manager is faced with a scenario involving interrelated systems, subsystems, causes, and effects. Unfortunately, the world is not so simple that a single change leads to a cause which, in turn, leads to an effect. For this reason, we explore here some of the variations that are necessary to resolve these more complex situations. There are basically three variations that need to be examined.

   1. *Start-Up Problems.* The analysis of problems that have been off track since day one of the expected performance.

   2. *Projective Cause Analysis.* The use of Cause Analysis in reverse— from cause forward to effect.

   3. *Causal Chains.* The hierarchical tracing of cause/effect relationships to a root cause.

Each of these variations requires a distinct manipulation of the standard process of Cause Analysis. Each of these variations will be discussed in turn.

Start-Up Problems

As we investigated the process of Cause Analysis, the key principle of "changes leading to causes" helped us to ultimately resolve the problem. This concept is dependent on a fundamental assumption: that the expected performance was observed at one time and the deviation began after that (see Figure 1.13). In Start-Up Problem Analysis there is no change from expected performance because expected performance was never observed at the expected level, as shown in Figure 1.14.

As Figure 1.14 illustrates, the problem performance has been in existence since the beginning of the activity. Thus, a search for change would be fruitless. We can, however, utilize the principles of Cause Analysis if we make some necessary modifications.

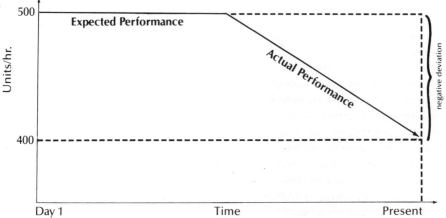

Figure 1.13 Deviation in Standard Cause Analysis.

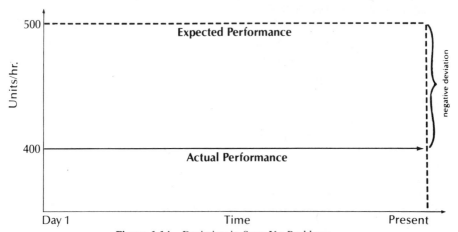

Figure 1.14 Deviation in Start-Up Problems.

STEP ONE. EXAMINE THE PERFORMANCE STANDARD

When a situation has been observed to be off track since day one, it is fundamental to assess the validity of the goals, objectives, or performance standards initially established. Goals are meaningless unless they are realistic. Establishing goals is easy. Establishing meaningful, achievable, realistic goals is difficult. Too often a target will be perceived as an end in itself and not subjected to a rigorous assessment to determine feasibility. The key question for the problem solver should be, "On what basis was this goal established?" The answer should reflect analysis of industry norms, prior achievement, lab test results, or some other method of goal determination.

For example, a new regional operation was established for a large research and development (R & D) organization. Since the branch lab had opened three years before, the turnover rate for lab technicians had been about twenty-five percent. The corporate turnover rate for that category of personnel had been fifteen percent, and this was seen as normal. The first key question was to assess the validity of the fifteen percent goal. Was it realistic to expect the same rate of turnover? In comparison to other organizations and based on reviewing the process for determining a fifteen percent expectation, it was determined that the objective was feasible, realistic, and not out of the question.

STEP TWO. SPECIFY THE VARIANCE

A Start-Up Problem can be specified using the same tools that we used in Cause Analysis: What, Where, When, How Much. The problem description should contain both the observed effect and the Comparative Facts to ensure precision. The difficulty in Start-Up Problem Analysis occurs in the generation of comparative data. There is no prior history from which to generate data for comparison. This forces us to go elsewhere, frequently to external systems, for our comparative data.

In our example of the regional laboratory, we might have had to look at other regional laboratories. If we hadn't had any others, we would have had to review the experiences of other organizations. The key to resolution is to search for comparative data. This is because there must be some reason for the unexpected results. The clue is found in the uniqueness of our regional laboratory. However, uniqueness requires comparison.

STEP THREE. COMPARE FOR DIFFERENCES

The key for resolving the Start-Up Problem lies in the isolation of key variables in the Differences step of the process. We have already determined that the cause will not be found in changes, thus our hope for solution lies in understanding how our situation differs from what was expected. The assumption is that two similar units produce similar results.

If there is no duplication of results then there must be something different in the operations of the two units. They are not truly identical. In our example of the regional laboratory, we would have had to utilize the two sets of data in our Observed and Comparative Facts columns. We would have had to seek out Differences by asking the question, "What is different or unique about the (1) unit, (2) location, (3) timing, and (4) extent?"

Perhaps some key variables would have appeared such as (1) the number of staff involved, (2) the limited levels of management for career development, (3) specific local market conditions for lab technicians, and (4) salary/cost of living differentials. The study of these different operating conditions now can be extended to theories of cause for the purposes of testing and arriving at the Most Likely Cause of the variance. The pursuit of cause is focused on the extension of Differences rather than on the search for and extension of Changes.

When facing a Start-Up Problem, a manager should recognize that there is a need to modify the use of the Standard Cause Analysis process. The key modifications are the following:

1. Question (in greater depth) the validity of the performance standard prior to analysis for cause.
2. Extend the search for Comparative Facts external to the system under study.
3. Suspend the search for Changes, and focus causal development on the Differences step of process.

Projective Cause Analysis

So far in Cause Analysis we have followed a process for investigating undesirable effects for the elusive "cause." Our analysis has been deductive and has required a distillation of data. While this is the most common form of analysis, it is not the only possible sequence. The manager frequently is forced into a very different cause/effect chain: the identification of cause followed by the identification of effect. While the basic principles remain valid and useful, the manager must be flexible in the use of them.

The need for this form of analysis can occur during the monitoring and controlling function of a manager's job. As managers scan key systems and key performance indicators, they frequently identify a situation that, judging by their experience, is worth checking out. The trigger for this concern can be either (1) a clear variance between performance and criteria or (2) the existence of a cause associated with an undesirable effect. This second trigger is the subject of Projective Cause Analysis.

In simple terms, suppose a manager knows that a certain cause usually produces a certain effect. When that cause exists, the immediate conclusion is that the expected effects either already exist or are forthcoming. For example, if an auditor knows that failure to invoice regularly (a cause) invariably produces cash flow interruptions (an effect), he or she must investigate cash flow every time an irregular invoicing system is spotted.

The manager can also be introduced to the cause by subordinates or others in the organization. In many instances subordinates describe causes or reasons for certain existing situations. The manager is thereby provided with a reason (a cause), for example, shortage of competent researchers. Prior to acceptance of this cause, the manager may have to verify the cause/effect relationship to differentiate between rationalization and valid reasoning.

STEP ONE.   TEST THE CLARITY OF THE STATEMENT OF CAUSE

Because the manager will be using the cause as a basis for exploring for effect, it is critical that its description be precise and defensible. The key test is for inevitability: Are the effects inevitable simply because the cause exists? The throwing of a large stone at a glass window inevitably produces shattered glass. However, a shortage of personnel does not inevitably cause a reduction of output. It is possible that people will work harder, change the work flow, lower standards, etc. Thus, the manager primarily must satisfy the definition of inevitability. If there is some question or concern about inevitability, the manager must reevaluate the continuation of the analysis.

A second test is for preciseness. To extend the definition of effect, it is critical for the cause to be singular and clearly stated. It is easy to extend and define the cause of "personnel shortage," but virtually impossible to extend and describe the expected effects of something as vague as "the combination of the hiring freeze and low-motivated employees in undesirable working conditions." The manager must ensure that the cause is defined singularly prior to extending the search for effects.

STEP TWO.   SPECIFY THE PREDICTED EFFECTS OF THE CAUSE

The same specification format used in Cause Analysis applies. The manager projects the expected effects in terms of what, where, when, and how much. The manager also should include a specification of expected exclusions or nonaffected areas (Comparative Facts). For example, a doctor uses this concept of cause/effect description when making a diagnosis. If a flu epidemic is rampant in a community, the doctor tends to begin diagnosis by assuming cause and validating the effect. The doctor will question the patient on what is wrong, what symptoms are being exhibited, what parts of the body are affected, when it began, the duration and frequency, and the degree or extent of the illness. Validity will also be tested by probing for other symptoms that should not be present, for example, dizziness. As long as the doctor gets negative responses to the nonexpected symptoms, he or she can continue to assume that the cause is flu. If the doctor begins to receive responses indicating that certain symptoms exist that don't fit the expected pattern, then he or she must question the cause/effect assumption and probe for other causes or compensating factors.

STEP THREE. VERIFY THE EXISTENCE OF THE EXPECTED EFFECT

Once the manager specifies what exact effects and exclusions are expected, then the situation must be examined to verify the existence of these effects. In simple terms, the manager tests to see if the facts fit the theory. This can be a difficult process. Because the manager is validating a predetermined theory, there is a danger of being selective in the data gathering. There is a tendency to find only those facts which support the cause and ignore those facts which reduce the validity of the relationship.

The outcome of this verification will be one of three conclusions:

Conclusion 1	It is true. There are the expected effects from the identified cause.
Conclusion 2	It is false. There are no observable effects despite the existence of the cause.
Conclusion 3	It is partial. There are effects, but not to the degree expected.

Conclusion 1: True.   If there now is a proven relationship between cause and effect, the manager assesses the seriousness of the situation and plans corrective action. In this instance the process is the same as Cause Analysis.

Conclusion 2: False.   If the manager cannot discover the expected effects, there are several other responses. Primarily the manager would reexamine the cause and ensure that the cause still exists and is still valid. If the cause has not changed or disappeared and still is valid in terms of inevitability, then the manager must search for the compensating control that must exist in order to explain the nonexistence of effects. In other words, the manager must find out what is breaking the traditional cause/effect chain. These compensating controls might be some conscious or unconscious activity or regulator aimed at the circumstance that prevented the existence of the expected effect. The identification of this compensating control is critical because it may enable the manager to do two things: (1) ensure that the compensating control remains within current procedures and systems and (2) recommend the extension of this control to similar cause/effect situations.

Conclusion 3: Partial Effects.   This conclusion is very similar to the last conclusion. The difference lies in the degree of observed effect. In this situation the manager discovers that most of the expected results are visible; however, the frequency or completeness of the results is not at an expected level.

In this instance the manager will search for contributing circumstances. Contributing circumstances affect the severity and magnitude and thus might be operating when partial effects are observed. In simple terms, something must be prohibiting the full operation of the expected cause/ effect relationship. Such circumstances reduce the impact of the cause/ effect chain.

Being aware of contributing circumstances, the manager can ensure that proper correction is made. Thus the role of contributing circumstances is recognized. The effects of these circumstances can then be increased or decreased within the existing system.

In summary, the manager's experience and knowledge should trigger analysis. The manager who recognizes causes must apply analysis to identify effects. This is a reversal of the usual process, which leads to cause from effects. The key to this form of analysis is the ability to project specific effects that inevitably result from an observed cause. This precise specification of cause becomes the data-gathering model for the manager to verify a particular theory of cause.

Causal Chains

A Causal Chain is a hierarchical list of the relativity of cause and effect. Unfortunately, the situations and concerns that managers face do not exist in isolation. As soon as we find the cause of one situation, we are faced with the need to assess the "cause of the cause." Frequently in Cause Analysis the identification of a Most Likely Cause simply triggers another focused Cause Analysis at a lower level. The need to find the root cause is the concern of Causal Chains.

The application of the Causal Chain process is the same as that of Cause Analysis. The difficulty lies in the concern for keeping track of where you are on the cause/effect chain. This variation can best be illustrated as an example.

You are general manager of a medium-sized manufacturing facility. Your secretary has just passed you a copy of a telex message canceling an order for one of your products. This was from a new client that you have been trying to sell for two years. The customer claims that failure to deliver is the cause of the cancellation.

Customer canceled contract

↑

Failure to deliver

As the manager your first actions are to verify the stated cause. A quick phone call to the inventory clerk indicates that current stock on the ordered product is high and that, according to inventory, the quantity was deliverable. A second phone call, to the shipping clerk, confirms that no shipment was made. The stated cause is thus verified.

However, as a manager you really are not any further ahead. The next step is to determine why no delivery was made when the stock was adequate and the product had been ordered.

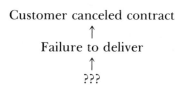

Customer canceled contract
↑
Failure to deliver
↑
???

You now have to move down the Causal Chain to plan corrective action. Another phone call, to distribution, reveals that they never received an order to ship the product. They have nothing on file.

Customer canceled contract
↑
Failure to deliver
↑
No order to ship in distribution

Having progressed to a lower level does not resolve the ultimate cause of the problem. So the cause, "no order to ship in distribution," becomes our new problem.

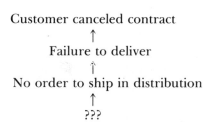

Customer canceled contract
↑
Failure to deliver
↑
No order to ship in distribution
↑
???

After several phone calls to track down the sales representative who sold the product, you discover that the sales rep phoned the order into the office from the customer's plant. To demonstrate flexibility, the new rep was anxious to get the product to the customer quickly. A few probing questions reveal that he did not follow up with a written order form. He still has that in his briefcase.

Customer canceled contract

↑

Failure to deliver

↑

No order to ship in distribution

↑

No written order from sales representative (phone call only)

As a manager you now have progressed down the chain to the point where you are in a position to prevent recurrence, or what we call Root Cause. While this contract may not be saved, repetition can be avoided by stressing to sales representatives that only written orders can be used for processing deliveries. Judgmentally, you might stop at that level. If you are concerned about whether this was an isolated occurrence or a failure across the entire sales force, you could extend to one more level. This would create a need to discover why the sales representative didn't process the written sales order. In this instance, the sales representative indicates that he didn't know that shipping required a written sales order. He assumed that if he called the sales office the paperwork would be done.

Customer canceled contract

↑

Failure to deliver

↑

No written order to ship in distribution

↑

No written order from sales representative

↑

Sales representative didn't know function of written order

The difficulty with Causal Chains is knowing when to stop. Eventually you come to a level of analysis where pursuing cause can be a waste of effort and time because you have gone beyond solving the problem. In our example a typical, illogical extension could produce the following:

Customer canceled the contract

↑

Failure to deliver

↑

No written order to ship in distribution

↑

No written order from sales representative

↑

Sales representative didn't know function of written order

↑

Inadequately trained in sales process

↑

President's nephew

Conceptually, Causal Chains are difficult because of the schizophrenic nature of each piece of data. Each level in our chain could be either a cause or a problem. Depending on where you enter the chain, you might have to go up or down the hierarchy. In our example, we made it quite simple by starting at the top and working back. However, a manager can enter a chain at any level.

For instance, the sales manager of the company in this example might notice that the sales representative has a few written sales orders in his briefcase and wonder why they have not been processed. This would cause the sales manager to apply the Projective form of Cause Analysis. The manager recognizes a cause and immediately projects up the hierarchy to predict certain effects. This could prevent certain problems before they occur.

A second difficulty in Causal Chains is the danger of progressing too quickly down the hierarchy without validating the cause at each level. In an attempt to get to the Root Cause, a manager can fail to verify that the cause at one level is truly the cause of the problem. This will create a logic gap, leading the manager down the wrong path. In our example the manager tested every cause/effect relationship before progressing to the next level. This ensures that jumping to cause is not legitimated in the Causal Chain.

CHAPTER 2

Decision Making

At some point, managers must progress from the analysis of past events to take action. Ideally, if the action is motivated by a proper analysis of the problem, we have narrowed our search for cause to the point where we can now confidently decide to "fix" the problem. It is critical to realize, however, that all actions are not motivated by a need to react. The underlying philosophy of this book is that good managers are proactive in their approach to problems. They continually take actions to improve situations, establish new directions, raise standards, and prevent problems that could threaten current plans.

The nature of uncertainty in this process is very different from that of the uncertainty in Cause Analysis. Though the time frame is the present, we are faced with a need to choose a course of action that will be implemented in the future. The dilemma is one of comparing the relative impact of alternatives without firm data. We will never know for certain what would have happened if we had chosen another alternative. The manager must review the alternatives and, with confidence, take a stand and declare that alternative X will meet our needs better than alternative Y or Z. This is, by its very nature, a difficult process.

The resolution of this uncertainty can cause some very interesting situations in organizations. One of the more fascinating is the confusion between "decisiveness" and "decision making." In many companies managers are assessed and rewarded on the speed and certainty of their decision responses. Uncertainty is not allowed to exist because it is seen to be symptomatic of weakness. Snap judgments are expected, and commitment to pursuing decisions in the face of adversity is rewarded. Though theoretically this is extremely laudable, it does not reflect reality as most managers know it. Decisiveness is the skill of making a decision and carrying it through. Decision Making is the process of analyzing critical data to determine the optimum choice. The blend of these two skills is important. The plea for decision making is not a plea for procrastination. Being paralyzed by analysis is as undesirable as making knee jerk decisions.

Like Cause Analysis, the Decision Making Process requires a logical and structured approach. We make decisions that require commitment and have to make them work. Once a commitment is made, it is difficult to reverse it and seek other options. It also stands to reason, however, that the steps of analysis for choosing between alternatives are going to be slightly different than those we take in analyzing for cause. Managers cannot follow the same steps in analyzing historical data that they do in analyzing present and future data.

A decision, as we defined it earlier, is a state of uncertainty which is caused by the need to choose a course of action that will achieve certain predetermined results. This "uncertainty" can take several forms:

1. The Standard Decision, where a limited, fixed range of alternatives exists.

2. The Binary Decision, where the alternatives are yes or no.

3. The Multi-Alternative Decision, where an excessive range of alternatives seems available.

4. The Innovative Decision, where action is required, but no alternatives are readily apparent or acceptable.

THE STANDARD DECISION MAKING PROCESS

In this book, we talk about methods of resolving the uncertainty of each of these decision types. The Standard Decision, however, will be our major focus for two reasons: First, this type of decision represents the most common form of decision making. It is always better to choose from a range of alternatives than to limit our choices. Second, the analytical steps involved in this type of decision also apply to the others.

In Cause Analysis, we recognize that the optimum use of our experience occurs in the causal development and testing stages. In Decision Making, our use of experience has to be included from step one and applied throughout the process. However, it must be controlled. In Cause Analysis, we have to be careful of managers' "pet causes." In Decision Making, we can fall prey to the preselection of "pet alternatives." In Decision Making, the preselection of a "pet choice" can bias the entire analysis, and the result will be a predictable selection of the "pet choice." The purpose of a structured approach to Decision Making is to increase objectivity and to ensure that we cover all essential data.

While Cause Analysis is a deductive process that forces a manager to gather facts then narrow them down (by the process of critical elimination), Decision Making requires that a manager build up a data base, which is then used to filter and eliminate less desirable alternatives. The end result is a single choice. It does not, however, have the solid, unquestionable "rightness" of the "true cause" of a problem. What we can do is reduce the number of alternatives to a point where the best choice is more easily made.

Basically, steps in the Decision Making Process are:

1. State decision purpose.
2. Establish criteria.
3. Separate criteria (limits/desirables).
4. Generate alternatives.
5. Compare alternatives.
6. Identify risks.
7. Assess risks (probability/seriousness).
8. Make decision.

Step One.   State Decision Purpose

Peter Drucker says in *The Practice of Management* (1969) that "it is more important for a manager to do the right things than to do things right."

Phillip Marvin, in *Developing Decisions for Action* (Dow Jones Irwin, Homewood, Ill., 1971), says:

Decision-making is based on the identification of worthwhile things to do. Decision-making is not an art—it is a process, and the most important part of the process is the indentification of worthwhile things to do.

Both of these writers emphasize the need in Decision Making to clarify the purpose of the decision. This is why any Decision Making Process must begin with a clear analysis of the need to make that decision and the relationship of that decision to other decisions.

Accordingly, before jumping into an in-depth analysis of choice, it is important to first ask some questions about the choice to be made. These questions serve three functions:

1. To show the relationship of the decision to the need to make a choice.
2. To give us direction in seeking alternatives.
3. To restrict alternatives that are outside our purpose.

Of the three functions, the most difficult and important is the relationship issue. Managers must make decisions. There is a feeling of achievement whenever uncertainty is removed. There is also a feeling of accomplishment in knowing that some action is forthcoming, which may give the comforting illusion that we are on top of the problem. Sometimes we fall into the trap of taking action without questioning the purpose of that action. For example, if a regional manager of a sales organization were to announce his resignation, the following decision would then have to be made:

1. Choosing a new regional manager.
2. Determining the most appropriate method of managing sales for that region.
3. Deciding who to promote.

These are three very different decisions. Decision no. 1 presupposes the continuation of the status quo. It does not deal with the possibility of reorganizing the regional sales operation. Decision no. 2 raises the level of the decision to the point where a wide range of alternatives is possible. However, if a conscious decision has previously been made to maintain the existing organizational structure, it is not valid or efficient to reconsider that decision. Decision no. 3 presupposes that the vacant position will be filled by a current salesperson. If the company policy dictates this decision, then it is appropriate; the nature of the decision statement determines whether lateral transfers or outside hires are considered.

The rightness of a decision purpose is determined, therefore, by its relationship to the situation to be resolved and to prior decisions. Thus, in attempting to assure the appropriateness of the decision purpose, a manager should ask three questions:

1. "What choice am I trying to make?" This question simply provides a starting point. It will be sharpened by two test questions which follow.
2. "Why is this decision necessary?" This question attempts to relate the decision to the situation being resolved, for example "Why are we deciding to purchase photocopy equipment?" If the response is "because the current machine is too old," you might want to find out if leasing or improving the maintenance contract on the current machine is also possible. As we observed earlier, there is always a range of reactions to a situation. It must be clear that the choice relates to the situation to be resolved.
3. "What was the last decision made?" This question relates to the concept that all decisions represent a chain of decisions. Locating ourselves on that chain is critical. For example, suppose a decision purpose was "To select a training program for implementation of the job enrichment program." Before we are able to proceed with this decision purpose, we must be able to answer the question: "Did we decide job enrichment would solve our morale problem?" And, if

so, "Did we decide that a training program was required?" Only with answers to these can we proceed, knowing that the prior decisions reflect proper analysis.

A proper Statement of Decision Purpose relates to the effects it will create and the effects it will resolve (if appropriate). It also should describe the end result desired.

Step Two.   Establish Criteria

Having determined that what we are deciding is important and being made at the right level in the logic chain, it is now time to begin the actual choice process. If a manager says, "That was a great decision you made six months ago," what is the basis of that judgment? There are two major aspects:

1.   Has what was supposed to happen really occurred? In other words, did the decision achieve the desired results?
2.   Did it achieve those results without an excess of adverse side effects?

Because decisions are judged primarily by their relationship to results, it is only reasonable to begin our process of choice by considering the results required. These are called our Decision Criteria. They represent the basis on which we will actually choose. Managers must have some concept of what they want to achieve. They must also have an idea about the resources available to achieve those results. In a structured approach, this step is triggered by a question. The key question here is "What factors should be taken into consideration in making this choice?" This question generates a shopping list of factors that must be considered in this decision. In a group situation, this would also ensure that those persons who are going to be influenced by the decision have the opportunity to specify their requirements.

An example of a decision might be more useful here than a discussion of sequential logic in the abstract. In our example, in which we follow all steps, we assume the role of the owner of a dry cleaning business: Having reviewed our profit/loss statements and the market potential, we have decided to expand and open a third dry cleaning store, including plant. The prior analysis produced a decision purpose—to choose a new site for a third dry cleaning store. A possible first run at generating criteria is shown in Figure 2.1.

Obviously, we could add many other factors. However, for purposes of illustration, these are sufficient.

The factors listed are fairly useless if we leave them at this level of generality. If they are going to be helpful as criteria for choice, we must convert them into concrete statements of requirement.

Before converting these criteria into specifics, it is worth considering that

STANDARD DECISION MAKING WORKSHEET

STEP 1. State Decision Purpose

To choose a new site for third dry cleaning store

Factors to be considered:

- Size of store
- Costs
- Location
- Parking
- Physical Layout

Figure 2.1 Analysis of Decision Purpose Statement.

at this stage a manager can very beneficially utilize others' help. In making a decision, we sometimes overlook individuals who will be affected by the decision and could suggest criteria that might increase the possibility of a choice. In this example, the store manager might suggest criteria to be considered. This is also the time to ask for the superiors' input. If the boss is going to review the decision, then it is necessary to get his or her ideas. This avoids the "Didn't you know about . . . ?" syndrome.

To make these general factors more specific, we simply assess each factor by means of the statement: "Whatever we choose should . . ." The completion of that sentence provides clear statements of Decision Criteria, as shown in Figure 2.2.

STANDARD DECISION MAKING WORKSHEET

STEP 2. Establish Decision Criteria	**STEP 3.** Separate Criteria	

Size of store
 	
  • Provide a minimum of
    4000 sq. ft.
Costs
 	
  • Cost a maximum of $17,000/year
Location
 	
  • Be in planning zone D4
	Limits	

• Located on a main artery–right-
    hand side for morning traffic
  • Be close to other stores
  • Provide maximum flow of
    pedestrian traffic
Parking
 	
  • Provide easy access for clients
Physical layout
 	
  • Wired for industrial use
  • Require minimum conversion
    for equipment
	Desirables	Value

Figure 2.2 The development of Decision Making Criteria.

Step Three. *Separate Criteria*

What we now have is a list of criteria, sufficiently specific to use as a basis for comparing our alternatives. However, each of the criteria has a different level of impact for us. For example, some of the criteria represent absolute and mandatory limits to our choice while others simply contain desirable features.

We live in a world where mandatory limits are a normal part of our decision making. Some of these are imposed by others and some are self-generated in an effort to assure certain minimal results. If the decision is to be effective, we must differentiate between the limits and the desirable features that may or may not be achieved. The key questions (again, the need for questions) are these:

1. If this criterion were not fully met, would the alternative still be acceptable?
2. Is this limit clearly measurable?

If we examine the list of criteria from our example, we can extract the limits shown in Figure 2.3.

STANDARD DECISION MAKING WORKSHEET

STEP 2. Establish Decision Criteria	STEP 3. Separate Criteria	
Size of store • Provide a minimum of 4000 sq. ft. Costs • Cost a maximum of $17,000/year Location • Be in planning zone D4 • Located on a main artery–right-hand side for morning traffic • Be close to other stores • Provide maximum flow of pedestrian traffic Parking • Provide easy access for clients Physical layout • Wired for industrial use • Require minimum conversion for equipment	**Limits** • Cost a maximum of $17,000/yr. for 3 years • Provide a minimum of 4,000 sq. ft. • Be in planning zone D4 • Located on a main artery–right-hand side for morning traffic	
	Desirables	**Value**

Figure 2.3   The separation of Decision Making Criteria into Limits.

For the purposes of our decision, let us say that any alternative must meet all of these criteria, there is no choice involved. "If a shop were less than 4,000 sq. ft., or over $17,000/year, or in other than D4, or not on the right-hand side of a main artery, we would be forced, by our own predetermination, to exclude that alternative from further consideration—regardless of what other desirable features the site may possess." These Limits remove any alternative that does not meet minimal requirements. This is necessary if we are going to restrict our search of alternatives to a workable list. For example, if employers advertise for a secretary, they need some basis for saying: "I'll interview only five out of forty applicants." Thus when Limits are used as a process of elimination, all other criteria represent desirable features.

We have now classified our criteria into two categories: Limits and Desirables. An additional step is to give some preference to those criteria we have categorized as only "Desirable." By definition, we do not give priority to the Limits. In management decision making, there are always trade-offs required. For example, will we trade off faster delivery for a better price? Will we trade off increased speed for better maintenance? A decision maker cannot avoid considering trade-offs. The key to good decisions is to identify the "Desirable" criteria in order of priority so that when trade-off time arrives, we trade off only in favor of important criteria.

The concept of separating Limits and Desirables has been around since time immemorial. This screening process is visible every day in newspapers. Job ads blare out the minimum requirements in an attempt to restrict the number of candidates who apply. The process of valuing Desirables is also common. Herbert Simon, in his 1948 text, *Administrative Behavior*, introduces a concept of weighted variables for administrative decision making.

There are many techniques for allocating value. The simplest is to use a base number valuation system. This is a simple process of choosing a base number for the highest-rated criterion and comparing the other criteria with that standard. Since North America is trying to implement the metric system, the number 10 is an easy number to use. Figure 2.4 demonstrates the application of this valuation system to our case.

The number represents the relative value and impact each Desirable should carry in the decision. When assigning relative values, the input of others is very important. This stage focuses the discussion on quantitative values and increases specificity.

To this end, we have created a specification of Limits and Desirables, giving a clear picture of what a good alternative should do. In the field of purchasing, for example, responsible purchasing agents would not consider the sources of supply until they had clarified their purchasing specifications. No decision maker should consider alternatives until the criteria are made clear.

STANDARD DECISION MAKING WORKSHEET

STEP 2. Establish Decision Criteria	STEP 3. Separate Criteria	
Size of store	**Limits**	
• Provide a minimum of 4000 sq. ft.	• Cost a maximum of $17,000/yr. for 3 years	
Costs	• Provide a minimum of 4,000 sq. ft.	
• Cost a maximum of $17,000/year	• Be in planning zone D4	
Location	• Located on a main artery–right-hand side for morning traffic	
• Be in planning zone D4		
• Located on a main artery–right-hand side for morning traffic	**Desirables**	**Value**
• Be close to other stores	• Currently wired for industrial use	10
• Provide maximum flow of pedestrian traffic	• Require minimum conversion for equipment	9
Parking	• Provide maximum flow of pedestrian traffic	7
• Provide easy access for clients	• Have parking available for clients	7
Physical layout		
• Wired for industrial use	• Provide maximum sq. footage	7
• Require minimum conversion for equipment	• Be close to other stores	5

Figure 2.4   The separation of Decision Making Criteria into Desirables.

Step Four.   Generate Alternatives

Because we are discussing Standard Decisions, this step is not difficult for the manager. By definition, Standard Decisions are characterized by a limited and fixed range of alternatives. In our example, we compare different site locations for a new store. A real estate office would be able to provide a list of comparable sites that could be used in our decision. As we explore other types of decisions, especially Innovative Decisions, this step becomes more complex.

Step Five.   Compare Alternatives

Good decision making requires a generation of a number of alternative solutions; the next stage is trying to compare these to make the best choice.

The dilemma of a manger facing a range of possible solutions can be likened to the proverbial child in a candy store. Sometimes all of them look good and none stand out as being significantly superior. To proceed, the manager needs some means for comparing the alternatives. Some of the tools that can be used for this comparison are now discussed.

The obvious starting point is to gather some information about the possibilities. In many instances, alternatives are initially described in very general terms; for example:

We can send all the work out to be done.
Or
We can hire temporary staff.

In order to be able to compare the alternatives, the decision maker first has to understand the choices being considered. For example:

How much will it cost to have the job contracted out?
Can it be done outside effectively?
When will it be finished?
Can we get approval?

Without sufficient data on our alternatives, we really are in no position to compare their relative merit. Consequently, we must first collect sufficient data on each alternative.

The task of gathering data about our alternatives is directly influenced by our list of Decision Criteria. The relevant data measures the degree of satisfaction on each criterion. Thus, the decision maker begins to gather data purposefully. The search is a planned process rather than a reaction to information as it surfaces.

Once a manager clearly specifies the alternatives, the concern becomes, "How do I arrange and compare the data?" Here a fundamental principle is necessary. Always relate the solutions back to the criteria. Never compare a solution with another solution. It is important to avoid "solution blindness"—an affliction that strikes managers who continually pursue alternatives and lose sight of the goals or the objectives.

Making a decision can be an end in itself for some managers. The feeling of uncertainty can be removed by simply deciding. But, to be effective, the choice must relate back to a purpose and to specific criteria. Solution blindness can cause a situation known as "Buyer's Remorse." This is the feeling that is best expressed by the phrase, "It seemed like a good idea at the time." Normally this is accompanied by a long description of the solution's appropriateness at the time.

The affliction "paralysis of analysis" can also be diagnosed at this stage. This occurs when the gathering of information about alternatives becomes an end in itself. Decision making is the process of making the best choice based on the best available data. There will never be a situation when all the facts are available. The process of relating alternatives to criteria is an attempt to assist the decision maker by focusing on key information sources. Both of the above decision maladies can be corrected by focusing on criteria rather than alternatives.

To illustrate this concept, it would be useful to refer to our "New Store" example and see what happens as we develop some comparative analyses to the various alternatives. The first step is to compare the alternatives of our Limits. We now gather data on each alternative and see if any can be eliminated. (See Figure 2.5.)

It is easy to determine that Site Three must be screened out because it fails to give us the required location in relation to traffic flow. All other alternatives meet our minimum requirements and so are still in the running.

The process of eliminating alternatives via Limits is a protective device for the decision maker. The alternatives that fail to provide minimum performance should be screened out early so that full attention can be paid to those alternatives still considered feasible. The Limits were created and determined by the decision maker and, therefore, must be managed by the decision maker. It is critical to continually reassess the validity of the Limits.

In many situations the list of criteria (including Limits) is created or developed in the initial stages of the decision making process. By the time the Limits are utilized by the decision maker, a significant period of time

STANDARD DECISION MAKING WORKSHEET

STEP 3. Separate Criteria		STEP 4 & 5. Generate and Compare Alternatives							
Limits		(Alternative A) Limits	Go/No Go	(Alternative B) Limits	Go/No Go	(Alternative C) Limits	Go/No Go	(Alternative D) Limits	Go/No Go
• Cost a maximum of $17,000/yr. for 3 years		• $17,000	Go	• $15000	Go	• $15,500	Go	• $15,000	Go
• Located on main artery–right-hand side for morning traffic		• Main rd.– right-hand side	Go	• Main rd.– right-hand side	Go	• Main rd.– left-hand side	No Go	• Main rd.– right-hand side	Go
• Be in planning zone D4		• D4	Go	• D4	Go			• D4	Go
• Provide a minimum of 4000 sq.ft.		• 4200 sq.ft.	Go	• 4000 sq.ft.	Go			• 4300 sq.ft.	Go
Desirables	Value	Desirables	Score/ Wt. Score	Desirables	Score/ Wt. Score	Desirables	Score/ Wt. Score	Desirables	Score/ Wt. Score
• Currently wired for industrial use	10								
• Require minimum conversion for equipment	9								
• Provide maximum flow of pedestrian traffic	7								
• Have parking available for clients	7								
• Provide maximum sq. footage	7								
• Be close to other stores	5								
			Total		Total				Total

Figure 2.5 Analysis of alternatives against the Limit Criteria.

may have elapsed. This makes it critical for the Limits to be reassessed for their current validity. For example, a manager might establish a Limit such as 15% growth in gross sales. A month later that Limit might be entirely unrealistic because of a market downturn or a competitor's action. Survival could be more important than meeting out-of-date limits. The concept of Limits in Decision Criteria guarantees that at least perceived minimal performance is met.

At this time, we take the remaining three alternatives and continue our comparison, using "Desirable" characteristics as shown in Figure 2.6. These facts represent the basis on which we can evaluate performance. The facts are the key. However, we still have to log our judgments about how well each meets our criteria.

We must now score our data relative to our Desirables. To do this, we simply ask the question, "Which alternative best meets that criterion?" That alternative receives a score of 10. The other alternatives receive a score based on the answer to the question, "How much better is the best alternative, compared to this one?" In our example, we see that our criteria specifies minimum conversion costs. It appears that Alternative One is the

STANDARD DECISION MAKING WORKSHEET

STEP 3. Separate Criteria		STEP 4 & 5. Generate and Compare Alternatives							
Limits		(Alternative A) Limits	Go/No Go	(Alternative B) Limits	Go/No Go	(Alternative C) Limits	Go/No Go	(Alternative D) Limits	Go/No Go
• Cost a maximum of $17,000/yr. for 3 years		• $17,000	Go	• $15000	Go	• $15,500	Go	• $15,000	Go
• Located on main artery–right-hand side for morning traffic		• Main rd.– right-hand side	Go	• Main rd.– right-hand side	Go	• Main rd.– left-hand side	No Go	• Main rd.– right-hand side	Go
• Be in planning zone D4		• D4	Go	• D4	Go			• D4	Go
• Provide a minimum of 4000 sq.ft.		• 4200 sq.ft.	Go	• 4000 sq.ft.	Go			• 4300 sq.ft.	Go
Desirables	Value	Desirables	Score Wt. Score	Desirables	Score Wt. Score	Desirables	Score Wt. Score	Desirables	Score Wt. Score
• Currently wired for industrial use	10	• Under construction. Could be wired as built		• No, store and retail only				• Yes, currently wired	
• Require minimum conversion for equipment	9	• Could be modified to suit $2500 for modifications		• No, would require $5000 to convert				• $3500 for modifications	
• Provide maximum flow of pedestrian traffic	7	• Near university –much pedestrian traffic		• Near shopping centers and park (yes)				• Near apartment complex–not much pedestrian traffic	
• Have parking available for clients	7	• Street parking only; limited		• Large lot behind store				• Street parking only– Lots of street space	
• Provide maximum sq. footage	7	• 4200 sq. ft.		• 4000 sq. ft.				• 4300 sq. ft.	
• Be close to other stores	5	• In small shopping center–10 stores		• Close to large multi-level mall				• 3 stores only in small mall	
		Total		Total				Total	

Figure 2.6 The listing of alternatives against the appropriate Desirable Criteria.

most desirable on this criterion because it meets our requirement better than either of the other two. We therefore assign a score of 10 to that alternative. The question now must be, "How much better is $2,500 than $3,500 and $5,000?" The expression of the importance of that variance represents the scores of Alternatives Two and Four. In our example we might score our judgments "7" and "4." Figure 2.7 shows the results of projecting this evaluation of relative performance across all criteria.

We now have a profile of individual performance against each criteria. To get the total picture of each alternative's performance (or "weighted score"), we would simply multiply the performance score against the value of the criterion. The assumption is that an alternative that performs well against a very important criterion should be given more credit than one which does well against a less important criterion. To do this, in our illustration, would give us the numbers indicated in Figure 2.8.

These totals, 394, 251, and 332, represent a profile of our judgment about the performance of each alternative. It gives us a snapshot of relative performance. It is not the sole basis for choice. It only tells us what is being performed in relation to criteria. It doesn't tell us what risks are involved.

STANDARD DECISION MAKING WORKSHEET

STEP 3. Separate Criteria		STEP 4 & 5. Generate and Compare Alternatives							
Limits		**(Alternative A) Limits**	**Go/No Go**	**(Alternative B) Limits**	**Go/No Go**	**(Alternative C) Limits**	**Go/No Go**	**(Alternative D) Limits**	**Go/No Go**
• Cost a maximum of $17,000/yr. for 3 years		• $17,000	Go	• $15000	Go	• $15,500	Go	• $15,000	Go
• Located on main artery–right-hand side for morning traffic		• Main rd.– right-hand side	Go	• Main rd.– right-hand side	Go	• Main rd.– left-hand side	No Go	• Main rd.– right-hand side	Go
• Be in planning zone D4		• D4	Go	• D4	Go			• D4	Go
• Provide a minimum of 4000 sq.ft.		• 4200 sq.ft.	Go	• 4000 sq.ft.	Go			• 4300 sq.ft.	Go
Desirables	**Value**	**Desirables**	**Score Wt. Score**	**Desirables**	**Score Wt. Score**	**Desirables**	**Score Wt. Score**	**Desirables**	**Score Wt. Score**
• Currently wired for industrial use	10	• Under construction. Could be wired as built	10	• No, store and retail only	0			• Yes, currently wired	10
• Require minimum conversion for equipment	9	• Could be modified to suit $2500 for modifications	10	• No, would require $5000 to convert	4			• $3500 for modifications	7
• Provide maximum flow of pedestrian traffic	7	• Near university –much pedestrian traffic	10	• Near shopping centers and park (yes)	8			• Near apartment complex–not much pedestrian traffic	3
• Have parking available for clients	7	• Street parking only; limited	4	• Large lot behind store	10			• Street parking only– Lots of street space	9
• Provide maximum sq. footage	7	• 4200 sq. ft.	8	• 4000 sq. ft.	7			• 4300 sq. ft.	10
• Be close to other stores	5	• In small shopping center–10 stores	10	• Close to large multi-level mall	8			• 3 stores only in small mall	3
		Total		**Total**				**Total**	

Figure 2.7   The scoring of the alternatives against the Desirable Criteria.

STANDARD DECISION MAKING WORKSHEET

STEP 3. Separate Criteria		STEP 4 & 5. Generate and Compare Alternatives							
Limits		(Alternative A) Limits	Go/No Go	(Alternative B) Limits	Go/No Go	(Alternative C) Limits	Go/No Go	(Alternative D) Limits	Go/No Go
• Cost a maximum of $17,000/yr. for 3 years		• $17,000	Go	• $15000	Go	• $15,500	Go	• $15,000	Go
• Located on main artery–right-hand side for morning traffic		• Main rd.– right-hand side	Go	• Main rd.– right-hand side	Go	• Main rd.– left-hand side	No Go	• Main rd.– right-hand side	Go
• Be in planning zone D4		• D4	Go	• D4	Go			• D4	Go
• Provide a minimum of 4000 sq.ft.		• 4200 sq.ft.	Go	• 4000 sq.ft.	Go			• 4300 sq.ft.	Go
Desirables	Value	Desirables	Score Wt. Score	Desirables	Score Wt. Score	Desirables	Score Wt. Score	Desirables	Score Wt. Score
• Currently wired for industrial use	10	• Under construction. Could be wired as built	10 100	• No, store and retail only	0 0			• Yes, currently wired	10 100
• Require minimum conversion for equipment	9	• Could be modified to suit $2500 for modifications	10 90	• No, would require $5000 to convert	4 36			• $3500 for modifications	7 63
• Provide maximum flow of pedestrian traffic	7	• Near university –much pedestrian traffic	10 70	• Near shopping centers and park (yes)	8 56			• Near apartment complex–not much pedestrian traffic	3 21
• Have parking available for clients	7	• Street parking only; limited	4 28	• Large lot behind store	10 70			• Street parking only– Lots of street space	9 63
• Provide maximum sq. footage	7	• 4200 sq. ft.	8 56	• 4000 sq. ft.	7 49			• 4300 sq. ft.	10 70
• Be close to other stores	5	• In small shopping center–10 stores	10 50	• Close to large multi-level mall	8 40			• 3 stores only in small mall	3 15
			Total 394		Total 251				Total 332

Figure 2.8 The weighted scoring of the alternatives against the Desirable Criteria.

Step Six. Identify Risks

As mentioned earlier in this chapter. a prime basis for evaluating decision effectiveness is how well adverse side effects that would reduce the overall effectiveness of the action were avoided. "The operation was a success—but the patient died." Good decision makers take a check step, called Risk Analysis, prior to finalizing choice. In most decision making theories, some element of risk analysis is included. It may range from the complexities of probability analysis in Operations Research Modeling to the gut level, "What do you think they'll do when we announce the price increase?" Our approach is closer to the last statement. We are concerned about a working tool for managers that can be used quickly and effectively and doesn't require mathematical sophistication.

Identification of the risk is based on two sources. As managers, we usually make decisions under time pressure. Consequently, we can often overlook criteria that later appear to be critical. Also, our increasing knowledge about alternatives frequently brings to light new information that could not have been predicted. In the identification of risk, we should look at both sources.

To apply risk properly, we should take one alternative at a time and predict those concerns we may have about that alternative's ultimate effect. The question, "What could go wrong if we choose Site One?" will generate some risks. In doing this, it is critical to consider one possibility at a time. What could go wrong with Alternative One usually has nothing to do with what could go wrong with the other alternatives. A few sample risks might be:

Site One—Tentative Choice
If building is not finished on time, then we will have to delay opening.

If the university business falls of in summer, then we will have cash flow difficulties.

These risks illustrate some typical side effects to be considered. The first should have been anticipated. Perhaps a criterion for availability should have been included. The second risk could not have been foreseen in the criteria but should be considered nevertheless.

Step Seven. Assess Risk

Knowing a risk is important, but it is not enough. We now have to apply some meaning to that risk. Every statistical assessment of risk considers two factors: probability and seriousness. If it is good enough for statisticians, we should be able to reduce it sufficiently for a workable, managerial application.

Probability attempts to describe the manager's judgment about the likelihood that an event will occur. Seriousness attempts to describe the judgment about the impact of that event if it did occur. To keep life as simple as possible, the same scale we used in our earlier process should be used. This gives us the following scale:

Probability	*Seriousness*
10—certainty	10—decision will fail
1—very unlikely	1—almost no effect

If we applied these assessments to our example of risks, in our judgment, we would have the results listed in Figure 2.9.

These numbers mean we predict a fairly high likelihood of not opening on time, and this will have a very adverse effect on our success. Our second risk is very different. The interpretation of P-9/S-2 is the low volume is almost inevitable; but its effect will be minimal, possibly because of the ability to reduce staff or manage the problem in other ways.

Since Site One was marginally better than Site Four, 60 points, the

STANDARD DECISION MAKING WORKSHEET

STEP 6 & 7. Identify and Assess Risk (note probability and seriousness)		
Alternative A	**P**	**S**
• If: Not finished in time (probability)	6	
• Then: Delay in opening (seriousness)		8
• If: Low volume in summer (probability)	9	
• Then: Cash flow problem (seriousness)		2

Figure 2.9   Risk Assessment of tentative choice.

decision maker would probably extend the risk analysis to Site Four. The profile of the risk attached to Site One is generally perceived to be significant enough to consider a second look at the next best alternative. In management it is sometimes necessary to accept a little less performance in order to assure a more positive implementation.

Step Eight.   Make Decision

The profile of risks helps us make a calculated decision. Now we have a picture with which to compare our profile of performance. These two pictures have to be assessed. The numbers in each profile have no relationship to each other, and there is no formula for equating numbers. The question now is "Is the performance I am obtaining worth the risk I am accepting?" One may be tempted, but should not multiply seriousness by risk. To do so can cloud the real issue. A 10×1 risk is very different in profile from a 1×10 threat.

We are not looking for minimal risk; we are looking for manageable and acceptable risk. In our example, Site One was better than the other two. It has one major risk, probable delay in opening. The decision maker might decide that this doesn't overshadow the performance, and thus decide on Site One. If, however, the risks are perceived as major, the relative risk to Site Four can be evaluated. The second-best in performance might be chosen because the risk involved is more manageable.

In making a choice, managers make a whole series of judgments. It is critical to log these judgments. The decision is a composite of value judgments. The process is very simple. It says:

1.   Know what you have to decide.
2.   Describe what criteria should be used to make the choice.
3.   Separate the criteria into Limits and Desirables.
4.   Generate the alternatives.
5.   Compare the performance of each alternative against the criteria.
6.   Identify the possible risks.

7. Assess the probability and seriousness of each risk.
8. Make the best-balanced decision.

A flowchart (Figure 2.10) and worksheet (Figure 2.11) are included here for further examination. A Standard Decision Making case study, *Corporation Commission,* allows the reader a chance to practice this process. A sample resolution is included in the Appendix. Practical applications of the Standard Decision Making Process follow the case.

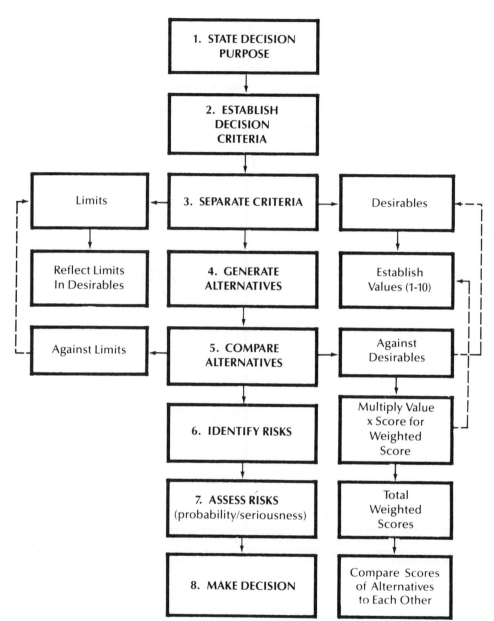

Figure 2.10 Flowchart demonstrating the steps in the Standard Decision Making Process.

STANDARD DECISION MAKING WORKSHEET

STEP 1. State Decision Purpose

STEP 2. Establish Decision Criteria	STEP 3. Separate Criteria	
	Limits	
	Desirables	**Value**

STEP 6. and 7. Identify and Assess Risk (note probability and seriousness)

Alternative _____	P / S
• If: • Then: • If: • Then:	

Figure 2.11 Worksheet outlining the

STEP 4. and 5. Generate and Compare Alternatives

(Alternate A) Limits	Go/ No Go	(Alternate B) Limits	Go/ No Go	(Alternate C) Limits	Go/ No Go
Desirables	Score/ Wt. Score	**Desirables**	Score/ Wt. Score	**Desirables**	Score/ Wt. Score
Total		Total		Total	

STEP 6. and 7. (continued)

Alternative _____	P / S
• If:	
• Then:	
• If:	
• Then:	

Standard Decision Making Process.

CORPORATION COMMISSION

A southwestern state in the so-called sunbelt of the United States is one of the fastest growing states in the United States. Over the last thirty years, its population has grown dramatically from less than 1,000,000 to 3,500,000. And, as new industries and retired people continue to come to the area, there's no let up in sight. Growth of this magnitude has created the usual growing pains—streets are inadequate, there are long waiting lists for installation of telephones, brownouts are frequent, and water supplies are often marginal. The situation is made even more acute each winter, since the largest industry by far is tourism. Literally millions of tourists swarm into the state for extended stays to take advantage of the state's dry, warm winter climate. Such an annual influx of people only makes the growing pains more severe.

In the early 1900s when it became a state, a constitutional convention was held. The state constitution which emerged was similar to other state constitutions in most respects. There is, however, one peculiarity in this state's constitution. Under the constitution, a fourth branch of government was created called the Corporation Commission. Comprised of five commissioners, who are elected by a general election every four years, the primary duties of the Commission are to regulate and administer the affairs of businesses operating within the state. Although the powers of the commission are broad, most of the functions for which they are responsible are perfunctory in that they entail such things as looking after the filing of articles of incorporation.

There is one responsibility of the commission, however, which is extremely important. This is the responsibility for establishing the rates of and licensing new facilities for all public utilities that operate within the state. Most of the commission's time is taken up with hearings concerning these matters, which are generally controversial since most of the residents feel that the rates are much too high and the service poor (due to the growth problems previously noted).

Whereas most states have commissions of this type, the difference in this state is that the commission is a product of the constitution, not created by the legislature. Accordingly, there is no way to control its activities or its budget other than by the vote of the general electorate who elect the Commissioners. Because of this high visibility and independence, the rapid growth of the area and at times the lack of qualified candidates for the office, the Corporation Commission has been the subject of much controversy over the years. Just recently, criticism of the commission and its activities has reached an all time high.

It seems that several years ago the commission set up a fund of money, the source of revenue being an assessment on all businesses operating within the state, based on the gross revenues of each company for any given year. The basic idea behind the fund was that it should be a sort of back-up, self-administered insurance fund which would reduce an individual company's liability in case of accidents or death on the job. Very few claims have ever been paid from this fund, as most companies maintain their own insurance. The primary usefulness of the fund has been its mere existence, which has helped to reduce the insurance individual companies have to pay. Although all companies have made contributions, by far the largest amounts have come from the public utilities whose revenues have been increasing rapidly due to the growth in population.

Over the years the amount of the fund has grown to $12,000,000. The ability to manage such a large sum of money without control by the other branches of government has been a source of temptation for the commission, exposing them to the possibility of graft and corruption. Indeed, in the early 1970s, an article appeared in the local press pointing out that in many ways the chairman of the Corporation Commission was one of the most powerful people in the state. This entire series of articles provoked the opposition party to institute a lawsuit. The suit was long and involved, but two and a half years ago the Supreme Court ruled that the existence of such a fund was constitutionally illegal. The court ruled that the commission had "overstepped its authority in levying what amounted to a tax," and therefore ordered the commission to divest itself of the fund.

As you can well imagine, divesting $12,000,000 is no easy task. (The opposition claims that the amount should really be $12,500,000; the commission denies that and states that there are $500,000 in unpaid insurance claims which must come out of the fund prior to divestiture.) At any rate, there have been many ideas set forth since the court's ruling, with many special interest groups trying to secure a part of the funds.

In addition, since the court's ruling, the state has experienced a number of natural disasters, the primary one being a series of floods which claimed several lives and resulted in washed out bridges, power failures, polluted drinking water, and broken sewers.

It is now summer, and the election is only eighteen months away. The governor positively does not want to face the electorate with the fund problem with all its unfavorable publicity unresolved. (The commissioners and the governor belong to the same political party.) Accordingly, the governor has contacted the commission and insisted on compliance with the court's order. A copy of the letter with the governor's suggestions is attached.*

---

*Although the commission is, in fact, an independent body, the governor is quite naturally the head of the party organization in the state and therefore has control over re-election funds.

FROM: The Office of the Governor

TO: The Corporation Commission

SUBJECT: Supreme Court ruling on divestiture of insurance fund

As all of you are aware, the Supreme Court of this state has ordered the commission to divest itself of the commission's insurance supplement fund. I want to reiterate to you our concern and how important it is that you respond to the court order immediately with your plan for disposition. Failure to comply in the most expeditious manner possible could create grave and legitimate concerns among the residents of our fair state.

Since this has been a matter of concern for some time, I have had several members of my staff submit proposals which they feel are potentially viable solutions. I submit them to you for your careful consideration. As you review these proposals, please keep in mind the percentage of voters represented by the retired persons in this state. Any proposal accepted should reflect their needs and interests. Naturally, we have the best interests of all the citizens of our state in mind. This office recognizes that no matter what alternative you might select, it is impossible to please absolutely everybody. Hence any viable alternative should allow the entire fund to be disposed of, but must not cost the taxpayers any additional monies. Your choice should have high visibility throughout the state—we want people to feel confident not only that the divestiture has been made, but also that the fund itself was intended for the public good. Since this is an election year, I think it advisable that the selected alternative work in favor of a positive party image for all concerned.

Regarding the disputed difference in the total amount of the fund, I believe that if the right alternative is selected, the people will not quibble over a few thousand dollars.

Which alternative would you recommend?

Alternative 1–Set up a Trust Fund

It is proposed that a trust fund be set up at one of the local banks. The income from this trust would be used by the commission to procure the services of professional consultants to prepare independent studies on problems which may be presented to the commission. It is felt that access to professionials and consultants in particular fields of expertise would greatly enhance the ability of the commission to perform its duties as defined by the constitution. Since the monies are already available, there would be general benefit to the taxpayers, that is, increasing the professional operation of the commission, without an additional tax burden to the individual taxpayer. In addition, the legal work necessary to establish such a trust would only take about six months to complete and the entire "insurance fund", down to the last penny, could be transferred to it.

Alternative 2– Construction of a Building at the Capitol Annex

It is proposed that the funds be used to construct a new building at the State Capitol Annex. Many complaints concerning the operation of the Corporattion Commission have come from the fact that its offices are housed in various places in the State Capitol. It is believed that putting all of its offices under one roof would greatly enhance the efficiency of the Commission. This would also make space available for other state operations. Land is available for such a building just south of the present capitol office building, and it would cost approximately $10,000,000 to construct. Plans could be finalized within a year and construction could be commenced thirty days thereafter. The new office could be occupied and paid for within two years. The additional $2,000,000 could be spent on landscaping, and creating a park-like atmosphere, giving the citizens a building they could be proud of. Construction would be performed by a local state contractor, thus providing jobs for resident workers.

Alternative 3–Rebate to Utility Payers

It is proposed that the funds be used to reduce the utility bills of the residents of the state. This would have the effect of a tax cut to those people who pay utility bills. We propose that a formula be worked out to determine the percentage of the total fund each utility has paid. This amount would then be prorated back to the user over the period of a year as a credit on their current utility bill. This would be very pleasing to most state residents and would also be highly visible since each month people would be reminded of the excellent job the Commission was doing to keep the high price of public utilities down. It is estimated that approximately $2,000,000 should be set aside for the administration of this program, with the remaining $10,000,000 to be distributed.

Alternative 4–A State-Wide Radio and Satellite Communications System

It is proposed that the monies be spent in establishing an earth satellite state-wide communications system. Recent experience during the floods has shown that a satellite communication system may have resulted in the savings of millions of dollars of property that would not have been damaged, as well as saving several lives. This is because a satellite system cannot be interrupted by natural phenomena or downed telephone lines.

Indeed, it is estimated that approximately one-third of the damaged property and lives lost could have been averted if a communications network such as this had been in place. Produced by a local industry, the total cost is $14,000,000. However, the company will reduce the price to the exact amount if the commission will agree to cooperate with the company in helping it convince other states that such a system is necessary. It will make our state a showplace model for the rest of the nation. The system can be installed in 12 to 15 months, and we can commit the monies up front. The company feels that with an in-place system to demonstrate, other states will follow, thus providing more jobs in the future. The benefit to the population at large is obvious, and the utilities specifically will benefit by improved communications and increased ability to control their field forces in repair operations. The system would be manned by the civil defense authority which is already in place.

COAL MINE OPENING

A coal mining company had to determine which new mine to open first. The president designated a group of fifteen managers, engineers, and other staff people within the organization to come back to him with a specific recommendation. The president had openly backed alternative C of three alternatives.

The group first considered the level of the decision statement, "To determine which mine to open first," and decided there was no need to adjust the level of the decision statement, either upwards or downwards. Given three alternatives and the time frame allotted the decision process, it was an adequate statement. To be certain though, they tested it with the president and two vice-presidents who were also involved in assessing the situation.

The group felt that in order to make a successful decision they had to consider all of the people and functions that would be affected by the final outcome. They first identified all the areas this decision would impact. This included purchasing, because they had to buy and get the equipment to the location; production, because they had to manufacture certain key parts; operations, because they had to provide a number of people and equipment to get the mine site open; industrial relations, because they had to locate a professional work force and a blue collar work force; legal affairs, because they had to make certain all the local, state, and federal regulations were being met and the permits had been filed, in addition to making sure all possible injunctions had been considered and avoided or resolved prior to the starting date; and many other functions omitted here. They then determined to what extent each function would be affected by the final decision. For example, they felt operations would be the highest impact area and the comptroller's office the lowest.

The group then interviewed the appropriate individuals in each of those areas to help establish the selection criteria for the decision. They asked people to list what this decision should accomplish in their area. The next step was to determine resources that were needed or seen as limitations in order to implement the decision. This was done for each function. Once the list was generated, they reviewed it and eliminated duplicate criteria (i.e., the same apparent criterion stated differently). The list was reviewed to ensure clarity and understanding. Each criterion was examined for accurate communication of intent. The group determined the measurement of each criterion; the final draft listed each of the selection criteria and indicated how it would be measured.

The group presented the list to the president stating, "These are the areas that will be affected by the decision and from discussions and interviews with the people in these areas or functions we have listed the following selection criteria." They showed him the original list and then the revised list. The president added several criteria and reinterpreted others. They debated the measurements of some, but in the end the list of decision criteria was firmly established.

The group took the list and went to the next step of the Decision Making Process, to separate the criteria. Some were Limits and had to be accomplished; others were merely Desirables. Once this had been done the group took a quick trip to the president's office and got his approval on those criteria they considered nonnegotiable limits. The group then weighted the remaining criteria giving the most desirable a ten and weighing the balance relative to that. They returned to the president's office for one last trip and got his endorsement on the weighting. The group compared each alternative with the Limits and all three alternatives passed. They compared each alternative with the Desirables and selected alternative A as the tentative choice.

They subjected the tentative choice and the next best choice to a thorough risk analysis. Alternative A was still the best choice given its positive attributes and balanced against its inherent risks. The group went back to the president's office and gave a full presentation in front of the president and board of directors. In forty-five minutes, they were able to get a solid endorsement from the president, the two vice-presidents, and the board of directors that alternative A would be the best choice.

SHRIMP INVESTMENT

A geophysics company generated an enormous amount of cash one year and was faced with deciding how best to invest that cash. A number of alternatives were reviewed. Finally, given their location on the Gulf Coast, the company decided to invest the money in a fleet of shrimp boats. A major effort was made to look into acquiring, outfitting, and operating shrimp boats, providing freezer capacity, securing contracts for hauling once the shrimp was harvested, and marketing.

The president of the company, reflecting on this decision, stopped the Decision Making Process long enough to ask the board of directors to rethink the purpose of the decision. The president recognized that having a firm grasp on the purpose of the decision permits the decision maker to select the best alternative. The decision, as initially stated, was to make the most money from the surplus cash over the next twenty-four months. Somehow it had evolved to "Let's get into the shrimp business." What was the real purpose behind the decision?

Another alternative was examined and selected. Rather than go to the expense of buying and outfitting shrimp boats, the company decided to buy smaller and less expensive boats as collector's items and then go out into the Gulf and purchase shrimp directly from the big shrimpers. The company payed full price for the shrimp, brought them back to their port, and sold them in the Northeast, Northwest, and Midwest at a price that more than recovered their cost and made a very tidy profit. As a result, they had invested very little capital in this alternative, compared to that required for buying shrimp boats (the other alternative), and the profits turned out to be better.

MANAGEMENT INFORMATION SYSTEM

A large government agency formed a task force to study, recommend, and plan the implementation of a Management Information System for the agency.

The task force comprised a range of members, including senior management users and technical experts from within the agency. The first task was to clarify the Decision Statement. Because of the various inputs this took at least two two-hour meetings.

Four subsequent meetings were required to develop a comprehensive list of Decision Criteria. The scope and dollar impact (10 million) of the decision caused this stage to be the subject of indepth discussion. A total of eight Limits and twenty-four Desirables was created. Typical criteria included these:

1. Capable of accepting input from 200 remote terminals.
2. Compatible with existing government hardware.
3. Providing electronic mail service facilities, etc.

The Limits from these Criteria were used to select three major suppliers who were given feasibility contracts to develop proposals based on the Criteria. When the task force finally received the proposals, the task force chairperson estimated that a $100,000 saving and a six-month leadtime reduction were due directly to the use of a systematic Decision Making Process in working with the task force and facilitating the selection of a supplier.

TEST EQUIPMENT PURCHASE

In a large electronics manufacturing plant, whose main business is developing and building specialized products to government order, the principal way of doing business is creating a series of project teams. The products are highly complex and therefore require a great deal of engineering and development and specialized testing on the front end, with only a minimum of thought and effort devoted to the manufacturing phase. Indeed, of the 4000 people employed at the plant, almost 3000 are highly trained engineers. Study after study has shown that the primary reasons these engineers stay at the company is that they very much appreciate the engineering challenge of their jobs and the work climate which is such that the "engineer is king."

Whenever a project contract is signed and brought into the company, it is immediately assigned a project leader and several engineers who report to the project leader. Needless to say, a strong feeling of camaraderie often develops between the various groups of engineers, and, also, there is almost an advisory relationship between these groups and their project leaders.

In this situation there was a brand new project leader who had been assigned a project, with six old-time engineers reporting to the project leader. There were several things working against this project:

1. It was the first project for the project leader.
2. The project leader was younger than any of the engineers.
3. The project leader was not an engineer by training.
4. None of the engineers had wanted to be pulled off their previous assignments and assigned to this one.
5. The project leader was a woman.

The question confronting this project group was what type of a certain kind of test equipment to buy. It seems that there were two processes which would do the job—one of these was mechanical in nature, and the other was chemical.

The project leader called a meeting to discuss this matter. Prior to the meeting all of the engineers got together and informally agreed that they thought that the chemical process was by far superior. The project leader, who was trained in the Decision Making process called her instructor because she had gotten wind that a prior agreement had been reached. As you would expect, the advice that she received from her instructor was, "Use Decision Making and stay in process."

She did. By conducting the meeting with the proper Decision Making structure and asking the right questions, the group soon realized that they had not done their homework, and that there were things they couldn't answer about how the criteria compared with the alternatives. At that point the new project leader adjourned the meeting and told the group to come back the following week when they had the proper information. This they did, and the meeting resumed, the leader using the original flip charts so that no time was lost going back over ground that had already been covered.

The decision of the group at the end of the second meeting? They unanimously adopted the mechanical process.

SETTING A MERGER AND ACQUISITION PROCESS

A few years ago while delivering a seminar for the top management team of one of our clients, we helped develop a merger and acquisition system for them using our Decision Making process.

The company did not have a systematic process for screening merger and acquisition candidates. Historically, their decisions had been based on individual alternatives that were presented by investment bankers or business brokers. In many instances, the possible acquisitions that were presented to them were from different industries, ranging in size from $5 million to $100 million in sales, and varying in profitability.

At the time of the seminar, our client's management team was planning to expand their company's operations by acquiring another company. Because of this, they felt a need to become more systematic in their search for a logical candidate. The management team knew that a great deal of time would be saved and the chances for a successful acquisition would be increased if they identified their Decision Making criteria before looking at alternatives. The Decision Making Process proved to be a valuable tool in this effort.

First, they established a Decision Statement that stated their desire to buy another company that would increase their company's long range potential for growth. Second, they established Limits for the candidates that they would seriously consider for purchase:

1. Must be in energy related industry.
2. Must be able to be acquired through an exchange of common stock.
3. Purchase price not to exceed $75 million.
4. Last five years earnings per share must have a 10% compound annual growth rate.
5. Facilities must be in the southwest region of the United States.
6. Must have a distribution system different from the one of parent company.
7. Must have ownership or control over energy resources (i.e., oil, coal, etc.).

Having established these Limits, they then screened the data bases of companies that passed this first test. At the same time, they gave this list of

Limits to the investment bankers and other organizations that had offered them acquisition candidates in the past.

After approximately thirty days of screening data bases of public and private companies; talking to investment bankers and brokers, they had a preliminary list of ten companies that passed the Limits Criteria.

They were now ready to score the Alternatives (the ten companies) against their Desirable Criteria. The Desirable Criteria was similar to the following list:

Management compatible with their own.

Possibly offering a revolutionary technology.

Would like plant and equipment to be new.

Would like company to be in oil exploration
with substantial reserves.

Would like the company to have as high a profit margin as possible.

Would like the company's corporate offices to be in Texas, Colorado, or California.

Would like the present ownership of the company to be private or control of the stock to be owned by a small number of people.

Would like the company's board of directors "friendly" to present company.

After scoring and comparing the ten candidates to these Desirables, two candidates whose score was very close remained. One had a score of 359 and the other had a score of 347. So the management team decided to take both candidates through Risk Analysis.

When the Risk Analysis was completed, they felt that one company would make an excellent acquisition; the other company came in a very close second.

As a result of this systematic process, the management team decided to aggressively attempt to acquire both candidates. This decision proved to be an important one because, as it turned out, their number one choice was unavailable at the terms (based on their Limits) they were willing to pay. However, their second choice was available and at a very favorable price. An acquisition eventually resulted from the offer.

The Plan Analysis Process also proved to be an effective tool for the implementation of the acquisition. After any major acquisition, many potential problems arise, like the possibility of key managers leaving the acquired company. Our client was prepared to prevent the potential problems from being realized. But, in the event that problems did arise, they were ready to implement effective contingent actions to minimize losses.

DECISION MAKING VARIATIONS

The process of Decision Making described in the previous section is appropriate for a vast majority of situations faced by managers. In most situations a known set of alternatives exists and the key task is differentiating relative performances. Unfortunately, one of the cruelest myths existing in management philosophy is that a single logical process "a process panacea," applies in all situations. As the natures of the alternatives differ, the requirements for an applicable process must differ. This principle initiated the separation of decisions into the various types referred to in the introduction of Standard Decision Making. The Binary, Multi-Alternative, and the Innovative types of decisions are explored in this unit.

The Binary Decision Making Process

A Binary Decision presents two diametrically opposed alternatives for consideration. The alternatives are usually competitive in nature and force a yes/no take-it-or-leave-it choice. These decisions rank very high on the anxiety and uncertainty scale. The extreme nature of the alternatives forces a decision maker or group to polarize and sometimes paralyze. When a decision is relatively clear-cut, and the alternatives are similar and aim toward the same purpose, the situation is fairly safe for the decision maker. The question is, "Which one meets our requirements best?" In Binary Decisions, however, that security does not seem to exist. Some examples of Binary Decisions are (1) Do I go on for an MBA at night school or not? (2) Do we open a third office or not? (3) Do I hire another salesperson or not?

As a basic premise, Binary Decisions reflect an unnatural state of affairs for a decision maker. The unnaturalness is characterized by the limitations on choice. The restrictions of yes/no, do/don't alternatives are very limiting. There are very few decisions that should be considered in these terms. It is our belief that most Binary situations are not being analyzed properly if they are left in the Binary mode. In our consulting experience, we have discovered very few valid Binary situations.

There are several reasons why managers paint themselves into a Binary corner:

1. A major cause of Binary Decisions is the upward delegation of decisions. It is common for subordinates, suppliers, or others who wish to influence the decision, to present the decision required in Binary terms. This attempt, either unconscious or conscious, is made to force a choice supportive of their position. If a decision maker is restricted in the alternatives being considered, there is a potential for stacking the deck.

Parents traditionally use Binary Decisions in an attempt to control and modify the behavior of children. Such comments as "Would you like to go to bed without dinner?" and "Do it or else!" are examples of restricting decision making by creating Binary Decisions. Subordinates who are trying to influence their boss's decisions do the same thing. "Boss, can I attend this three day course in Chicago?" If the boss accepts the decision in this form, he or she now has a Binary choice.

A consequence of leaving a decision in this form is to increase the inevitability of a win-lose situation. These decisions are usually labeled "opportunities." Such labeling places pressure on the decision maker to accept the type of decision as Binary and thus restrict the choice. Salespersons are trained to present alternatives in the form of opportunities as a technique to manipulate the buyer. The acceptance of a situation as an opportunity increases the probability of the buyer accepting the proposal.

2. Second, Binary Decisions are not created from a manipulative mode, but rather are a result of *Superficial analysis*. Because tradition, history, and habit are so ingrained in most organizations, there is a tendency not to open up decisions to the conscious consideration of a wide range of alternatives. Questioning whether there are different ways to achieve the same ends is not seen as healthy, socially acceptable behavior in many organizations. As a result, Binary Decisions become a way of life. "Do we do it or not?" The consideration of the decision is predicated on the existence of one known alternative. If that is decided on, nothing is changed.

3. A third reason for the existence of Binary Decisions is time. Under the pressures of time, it is frequently quicker to simply decide on a course of action rather than explore the validity of the decision. Decisiveness is an admired trait in modern management. The high profile ability to accept responsibility for saying "Yes" or "No" is one that is cultivated and rewarded.

The danger of excessive rewards for decisiveness is that it can soon replace decision making. Making a decision, to be seen making a decision, can become an end in itself. Proper analysis of facts becomes labeled plodding and over-cautious. In these instances Binary Decisions become perceived as high profile, decisive examples of a manager's effectiveness.

4. Valid Binary Decisions can exist. There are instances where the manager has progressed along the decision chain and reached the lowest decision level: yes or no. In our experiences this has usually occurred following a series of consciously made decisions and is a concluding decision in a chain of events. An example of a valid Binary is a Make or Buy Decision. This is particularly true when dealing with a single source situation.

Because of the competitive nature of the alternatives, it is clear that an application of Standard Decision Making techniques leads to frustration. It is necessary to modify the standard process to accommodate Binary Decisions.

It is essential to begin by stating as clearly and simply as possible the intention of making the decision. Make sure that it is Binary and not just worded incorrectly.

It is virtually impossible to know how to handle any decision if you do not understand how you arrived at the Decision Making point. We looked at four reasons or causes for being in a Binary situation. If any of the first three causes (manipulation, superficiality, or time pressures) exists, it is critical to assess the validity of the Binary mode. The questioning of the Binary validity is done by reviewing the Decision Purpose.

Since the existence of the Binary Decision has been made evident by the Decision Purpose, we must consider changing that if we want to change the nature of our decision. A basic pressure is to "whenever possible attempt to get the decision out of the Binary mode." All decisions exist as part of a chain of decisions. A Binary Decision reflects the absolutely lowest level of decision in a chain. It is a go/no go point. If we want to avoid this forced choice, we have to change or elevate the level of the decision.

For example, if a decision purpose is phrased "Do I go to Chicago to take this course?" it is very restricting. You have only two choices: going or not going. If we examined the statement by using the questions from the unit on Standard Decision Making, we might be able to modify the statement to increase the range of alternatives and thus make a more objective decision. The questions follow:

1. Why is this decision necessary? Why do you want to go to the course? What problems will it solve? What skills will it develop? These questions will attempt to force the consideration of a cause/effect relationship between the decision and the need for any decision.

2. What was the last decision made? This question will attempt to track this decision in accordance with prior decisions. In this instance, an acceptable answer would be "There is a need to learn some skills and a course is the right way to do it." If that decision has not been made, then perhaps we should back off from the present decision.

We could then change our statement from "Do I take this course in Chicago or not?" to "How can I best learn the skills required to improve my performance?"

Going to Chicago and taking a course is still an alternative; however, we have opened up a wider range of alternatives, such as on-the-job training, other courses, job assignments, university/technical courses, etc.

This decision becomes easier to make and standard techniques can be applied to differentiate the relative performance of the alternatives. These preliminary steps have tried to change the Decision Purpose to a more open decision. This will not always be possible.

Despite the attempt to take decisions out of a Binary mode, there will be instances where it will not be possible. Hopefully this will be because they are valid Binary choices. The existence of two competitive alternatives places increased pressure on the Decision Criteria. The tendency is to simply list the pros and cons of each alternative and see if they cancel each other out. This can lead to difficulty because normally in a Binary Decision there are proponents for each side of the coin.

Basically the same steps used in Standard Decision Making are applied, though they have to be developed more critically. The key step is the development of criteria. Since the decision will be made based on the criteria, it is imperative that the decision maker not subjectively bias the list of criteria. For example if the decision were "Do I go to Europe this fall or not?", we could create a list of criteria as follows:

Should be as exciting as possible.

Expand my horizons.

Be educational for the family.

Broaden our exposure to different cultures.

Support and extend the second language skills of the family.

It is obvious that this is a biased set of criteria. There is no question of the decision maker's going to Europe. It appears that the Desirable Characteristics of one alternative (going) have all been included and the Desirable Characteristics of staying (i.e., costs, time, home improvements, etc.) have all been omitted.

To make a Binary Decision properly, the list of criteria should avoid data that describes only one alternative. If it is essential to include data about one alternative, you should compensate by including data about characteristics of the other alternative. To do so increases the objective framework.

To develop the list of criteria, many managers recommend that the positive and negative features of both alternatives be listed. These are really the pros and cons of each course of action. From these lists, the criteria can be developed to ensure that a complete and objective picture has been established. It is difficult to make the decision based simply on pros and cons. They do not necessarily cancel each other out and thus need some conversion process to assist the decision maker.

Previously in this chapter, we illustrated the process of Standard Decision Making with the dry cleaning store example. Since this data is relatively familiar, we will continue with this example in the Binary Decision.

Binary Example

The new store is open and everything is progressing on schedule. Business is growing slowly and the new equipment is functioning remarkably well. When purchasing the equipment, there was an intentional over-capacity planned into the store. As a result, the washers, cleaners, and dryers are underutilized at present. Several new decisions can now be approached by a manager for the purposes of our illustration.

> Decision No. 1   Do we add pick-up and delivery service?
>
> Decision No. 2   Do we bid on a contract for office building drapes?

Decision No. 1

The key first step in our Binary Decision is to explore the issue of cause. Why are we in a Binary Decision? If we ask the key questions of our Decision Purpose, we discover the following:

Why do we need to pick up and deliver? The answer is to increase our gross volume and expand beyond the current geographical area. Further questions such as, "What was the last decision made?" and "What other alternatives were considered?" reveal that no other thinking had occurred and we are really unnecessarily involved in Binary Decision.

The key next step is to elevate that decision purpose to a higher level statement, for example, "How can we best increase volume?" With this decision purpose, we can explore a wider range of alternatives—advertising, weekly specials, pick-up and deliver, plus a host of other viable possibilities. We can then apply a Standard Decision Making Process and determine which alternative will provide the best overall performance.

Decision No. 2

Do we bid on the contract for office drapes? For illustration purposes, we will assume that this is a valid Binary. It is an opportunity that has been created. It is strictly yes/no and it is at the lowest level in the decision chain.

The first step is to list the positive and negative results that would accrue from each alternative. This list of pros and cons can be used as a source for our decision criteria. A possible list of pros and cons appears in Figure 2.12.

Many managers identify only the pluses and minuses of the two alternatives. However, the pros and cons cannot determine the final decision, unless it is obvious that no further analysis is required. They are, however, a fruitful source of Decision Criteria, which can be a basis for choice. Using this list of positive and negative results, we can now develop a working list of criteria. The same principles of criteria development discussed in Standard Decisions apply. The statement "Whatever we do should . . ."

BINARY DECISION MAKING WORKSHEET

STEP 2. Generate Potential Results	STEP 3. Establish Decision Criteria
Yes Alternative: Bid on commercial contract	
Potential Positive Results	
• Increased volume in cleaning • Increased dollars of profits • Potential evening out of workload	
Potential Negative Results	
• Need to post bond–ties up cash • Evening work is involved–drapes have to be removed and hung up after working hours • Need to rent a truck • Less % of profit per unit • Industrial clients do not pay as quickly • Could interfere with current business	
No Alternative: Don't bid on contract	
Potential Positive Results	
• Maintain flexibility to grow in consumer dry cleaning • Minimize evening work • Maintain profit margin (%)	
Potential Negative Results	
• If we don't bid, we might get removed from source of lists and not be able to bid on other contracts • If non-industrial business takes longer to develop, machine utilization will stay down	

Figure 2.12   A sample list of expected positive and negative results identified in Binary Decision Making.

defines the Decision Criteria. The criteria that might result from probing this preliminary listing of pros and cons are found in Figure 2.13. These criteria have been separated into Limits and Desirables as in the Standard Decision Making process.

These criteria can now be applied to assess the relative performance of the alternatives, Yes and No. The process of comparison is the same as in

BINARY DECISION MAKING WORKSHEET

STEP 4. and 5. Separate Criteria and Compare Yes/No Alternatives

Limits		Yes Alternative	Go/ No Go	No Alternative	Go/ No Go
• Maintain a profit margin of at least 14%					
• Not interfere with normal same day service of current customers					
Desirables	**Value**	**Desirables**	Score/Wt. Score	**Desirables**	Score/Wt. Score
• Increase machine utilization	10				
• Provide business for slack periods	9				
• Not restrict growth of current business	9				
• Minimize additional evening work	7				
• Increase gross profit	7				
• Minimize additional cash outlay	5				
		Total		**Total**	

Figure 2.13   List of Criteria resulting from expected pros and cons.

Standard Decision Making. Figures 2.14 and 2.15 illustrate the comparison stage of analysis.

In our example we now see that the Yes alternative seems to be slightly preferable to the No alternative. Of particular significance is the application of scores in reviewing the Desirables. There is a 10-0 score on only one particular Desirable. Even though several times the better alternative

BINARY DECISION MAKING WORKSHEET

STEP 4. and 5. Separate Criteria and Compare Yes/No Alternatives

Limits		Yes Alternative (accept contract)	Go/ No Go	No Alternative (refuse contract)	Go/ No Go
• Maintain a profit margin of at least 14%		• 14 %	Go	• 16% is current return	Go
• Not interfere with normal same day service of current customers		• Possibly on some exceptional days but not normally	Go	• No impact	Go
Desirables	**Value**	**Desirables**	Score/Wt. Score	**Desirables**	Score/Wt. Score
• Increase machine utilization	10				
• Provide business for slack periods	9				
• Not restrict growth of current business	9				
• Minimize additional evening work	7				
• Increase gross profit	7				
• Minimize additional cash outlay	5				
			Total		Total

Figure 2.14   Decision Criteria Limits and evaluation of YES/NO alternatives.

received a 10, there was no need to completely ignore the performance of the other alternatives. Thus if one alternative receives a score of 10 on a particular Desirable, the other alternative should still be considered in relative terms and ranked accordingly. It is important to minimize the number of 10-0 scores because the resulting impact on the total decision score may be greater than that particular Desirable warrants.

Because the potential negative results were generated in the prelisting of

BINARY DECISION MAKING WORKSHEET

STEP 4. and 5. Separate Criteria and Compare Yes/No Alternatives

Limits		Yes Alternative (accept contract)	Go/ No Go	No Alternative (refuse contract)	Go No Go
• Maintain a profit margin of at least 14%		• 14 %	Go	• 16% is current return	Go
• Not interfere with normal same day service of current customers		• Possibly on some exceptional days but not normally	Go	• No impact	Go

Desirables	Value	Desirables	Score Wt. Score	Desirables	Score Wt. Score
• Increase machine utilization	10	• Would increase to 70% for one month	10 100	• No effect– current 50%	6 60
• Provide business for slack periods	9	• If contracts come at right time (consider risks)	10 90	• No effect	8 72
• Not restrict growth of current business	9	• Could if business grew in commercial contracts	7 63	• No restriction	10 90
• Minimize additional evening work	7	• Additional 2 hours 3 times/ week for 1 month	5 35	• No additional time	10 70
• Increase gross profit	7	• Additional $4000 profit	10 70	• No change to gross dollars	0 0
• Minimize additional cash outlay	5	• Post bond ($1000) plus truck rental	6 30	• No cash required	10 50
		Total	378	**Total**	342

Figure 2.15   Decision Criteria Desirables and evaluation of YES/NO alternatives.

Decision Criteria, there can be a tendency to ignore risks. This is dangerous for a decision maker and should be monitored. Risks can still exist. The generation of data about both alternatives might reveal some new potential negative results that should be considered. The application of risk analysis is as critical in Binary Decisions as it is in standard comparison decision.

The same method of indicating probability and seriousness used in Standard Decision Making is applied here also.

In our illustration we are only trying to demonstrate the variations of Binary Decisions, not risk analysis. Thus, we will assume that the Yes option seems to be our logical choice. The key data to check to guarantee success would be the scheduling of the contract to ensure it does not interfere with current, same-day service.

In summary, Binary Decisions are different from other types of decisions because they force a decision maker to operate in a restricted manner. The polarization created by the nature of the alternatives can result in data being biased rather than objective. In all instances a manager or group should attempt to change the decision being made from a Binary to a standard type of decision. When a Binary Decision is truly necessary, the steps suggested here and in the flowchart (Figure 2.16) and worksheet (Figure 2.17) can be useful in determining the final choice.

The Multi-Alternative Decision Making Process

Just as being unnecessarily restricted in making decisions leads to frustration, so the opposite can be frustrating. There are times when the number and range of alternatives seem endless. The Standard Decision Process suggests that the manager create a set of criteria and then compare the performance of every alternative with every other alternative. Can you imagine 300 alternatives laid out in a row for cross comparison! This is hardly viable or even desirable. For this reason, it is necessary to modify the information processing technique for Decision Making. While the multi-alternative variation does not occur frequently, it is worthy of consideration. A manager will often abandon the use of the logical process when the variation causes a feeling of futility. Rather than abandoning the process, managers can modify it.

The first two steps in this type of decision are exactly the same as in Standard Decision Making: develop a statement of decision purpose and create a list of criteria to be used in making the decision. These criteria should be classified into Limits and Desirables and the Desirables assessed in terms of relative value. This process is especially valuable if a manager does not want to eliminate alternatives with the Limits.

The variation required for this type of decision is introduced at this stage. Obviously, the criteria cannot be used for determining relative performance, that is, which alternative best meets the criteria in relation to the others. The physical task of comparing fifty or more alternatives would be overwhelming. What is required is conversion of this list into an absolute scale so that each alternative can be scored as a single entry.

To illustrate the process of Multi-Alternative Decision Making, let us extend the earlier example of the thriving dry cleaning business.

Multi-Alternative Example

While we are not exactly conquering the world, business is growing. We have reached the point where we need to hire an additional person as front

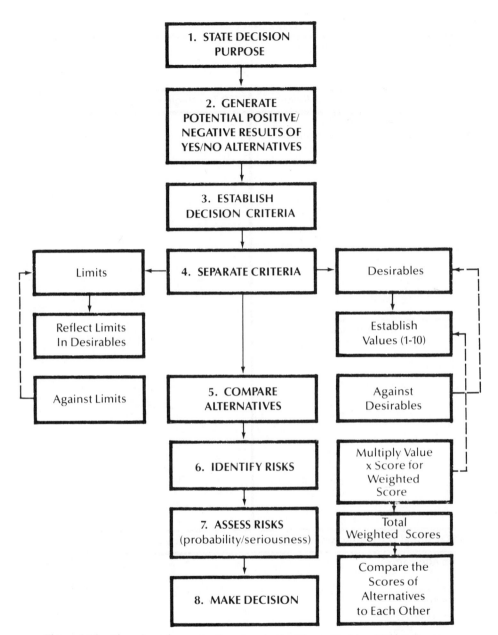

Figure 2.16 Flow chart demonstrating steps in the Binary Decision Making Process.

BINARY DECISION MAKING WORKSHEET

STEP 1. State Decision Purpose

STEP 2. Generate Potential Results	**STEP 3.** Establish Decision Criteria
Yes Alternative (potential pos./neg. results)	
No Alternative (potential pos./neg. results)	

STEP 6. and 7. Identify and Assess Risk (note probability and seriousness)

Yes Alternative	**P / S**
• If: • Then: • If: • Then:	

Figure 2.17 Worksheet outlining the steps

STEP 4. and 5. Separate Criteria and Compare Yes/No Alternatives

Limits		Yes Alternative	Go/ No Go	No Alternative	Go/ No Go
Desirables	**Value**	**Desirables**	Score/ Wt. Score	**Desirables**	Score/ Wt. Score
		Total		**Total**	

STEP 6. and 7. (continued)

No Alternative	P / S
• If: • Then: • If: • Then:	

in the Binary Decision Making Process.

desk cashier and laundry receiver. This is basically an unskilled job and the range of high school students, relatives, friends of friends, and others seem overwhelming. We know that an advertisement in the paper will yield an unworkable number of applications. Our concern lies in not wanting to hire the first person who comes along and yet we are not able to interview all fifty.

The process of defining and ranking criteria is demonstrated in Figure 2.18. This list is simply for the purposes of this illustration and could be extended as appropriate for a real situation. The Limits are of prime value in this kind of decision. The function of a Limit is to screen out unacceptable performers. In this example, we wouldn't bother interviewing anyone who failed to meet our three Limits. These could be used in an advertisement or over the phone in handling inquiries. These could also be

MULTI-ALTERNATIVE DECISION MAKING WORKSHEET

STEP 2. Establish Decision Criteria	STEP 3. Separate Criteria	
	Limits	
	Desirables	Value
	• Prior experience in dry cleaning	10
	• High school education	6
	• Bilingual to meet local customer needs	8
	• Pleasant customer relation attitude	7
	• Prior cash handling experience	5
	Total Value	_____
	Ideal Score (total value x 10)	_____
	Minimum Score	

Figure 2.18   Criteria defined and ranked for a Multi-Alternative Decision.

delegated to others to reduce the number of alternatives to a more workable range.

When making a Multi-Alternative Decision, the method of assigning values to the Desirables is the same as it is in Standard Decision Making. The most important Desirable is given the highest number (e.g., 10) and the others are ranked relative to it.

The difficulty of Multi-Alternative Decisions occurs in the use of the Desirables. Our traditional use of Desirables has been to determine relative performance of the alternatives. This is not feasible in a situation where we see one alternative at a time and have a long list of possibilities. To overcome this difficulty we modify our use of the Desirables from relative measures to absolute measures. What this means is that we will assess each alternative individually and score its performance against a theoretical ideal rather than against the performance of other alternatives. To do this the manager takes the list of criteria and totals the sum of the values, as shown in Figure 2.19.

This total is now multiplied by 10. The score 10 represents the score that would be attributed to a theoretically ideal alternative. Thus, an ideal alternative would score 10 on each criteria. Our own example could generate a theoretically perfect score of $36 \times 10 = 360$. This number represents a perfect alternative that is ideal against each criteria. It is unlikely that that alternative exists; however, it provides a basis for comparing the performance of each alternative.

The decision maker now assesses each alternative against every criterion and ascribes a performance score that represents how close the alternative comes to the ideal. Thus, a candidate might score 8 out of 10 in terms of attitude toward customers and be given a score of 56 (value of criteria × score).

At the end of this assessment, each candidate's total score could be compared to two different figures:

1. *Ideal Performance.* How close the individual comes to exactly what the decision maker was looking for.
2. *Minimum Performance Level.* The decision maker might determine a minimum acceptable score, for example, a passing grade of 250 out fo 360. This method of looking at individual alternatives allows the decision maker to quickly assess performance without waiting to arrange all the alternatives in one information matrix.

In this manner, we can convert relative decision making techniques into operational absolute scales to cope with a wide range of alternatives. While it is helpful to establish the ideal performance score, the more important quantitative measure is the minimum performance level. Since each alternative will be evaluated separately on its own merit, rather than in direct comparison to others, it is necessary to determine the minimum score acceptable before reviewing the various alternatives.

MULTI-ALTERNATIVE DECISION MAKING WORKSHEET

STEP 2. Establish Decision Criteria	STEP 3. Separate Criteria	
	Limits	
	• Be available for work no later than June 1 • Accept minimum wage of $3.75/ hour • Be willing to work Saturdays	
	Desirables	**Value**
	• Prior experience in dry cleaning	10
	• Bilingual to meet local customer needs	8
	• Pleasant customer relation attitude	7
	• High school education	6
	• Prior cash handling experience	5
	Total Value	36
	Ideal Score (total value x 10)	360
	Minimum Score	

Figure 2.19   Total the values of the Desirable Criteria and then multiply by the number 10 to establish ideal performance.

If a number of candidates were still close and under consideration, the manager would simply revert to a Standard Decision Making model with the now workable list of alternatives. A flowchart (Figure 2.20) and worksheet (Figure 2.21) provide further assistance in using the Multi-Alternative Decision Making Process.

The final three steps of the process are the same as in Standard Decision Making: Identify Risks, Assess Risks, and Make the Decision.

The Innovative Decison Making Process: Criterion Optimization Technique

The three types of decision making we have covered are all rational by nature. They represent techniques for sorting out masses of fact and evaluating data. In Innovative Decision Making, we are presented with a

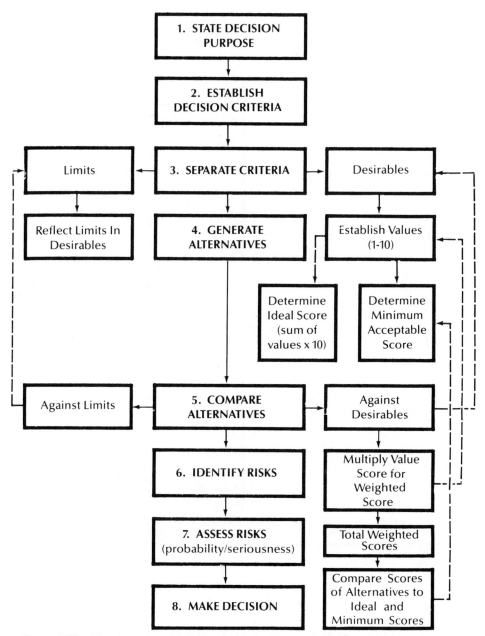

Figure 2.20 Flowchart demonstrating steps in the Multi-Alternative Decision Making Process.

MULTI-ALTERNATIVE DECISION MAKING WORKSHEET

STEP 1. State Decision Purpose

STEP 2. Establish Decision Criteria	STEP 3. Separate Criteria	
	Limits	
	Desirables	**Value**
	Total Value	
	Ideal Score (total value x 10)	
	Minimum Score	

STEP 6. and 7. Identify and Assess Risk (note probability and seriousness

Alternative	P / S
• If:	
• Then:	
• If:	
• Then:	

Figure 2.21 Worksheet outlining steps in the

STEP 4. and 5. Generate and Compare Alternative(s)

Alternative	Limits	Go/ No Go

	Desirables	Score/ Wt. Score
	Alternative Score	
	Minimum Score	

STEP 6. and 7. (continued)

Alternative	P / S
• If: • Then: • If: • Then:	

Multi-Alternative Decision Making Process.

decision that has to be made without any readily apparent alternative. As we move to Innovative Decisions now, we must change the use of the brain from rational to creative. We must use what is known as the right brain rather than the left brain.

The difficulty of effective alternative generation lies in the need to combine some rational processes, move to a creative process, and then return to a rational process. It is this phasing in and out that causes difficulty. Even creative processes have to be structured within some framework to be useful. A fallacy exists that groups have to be either creative or rational. These approaches are treated as opposite ends of the spectrum. In fact, groups have to be able to operate in both modes to be effective. The totally nongoal-oriented creative think tanks are a luxury most managers cannot afford on an ongoing basis. Good creativity is goal-oriented and is focused on specific concern resolution.

A superficial comparison of rational and creative processes would show the similarities and the differences, as indicated in Figure 2.22

This overview indicates similarities and highlights differences between rational and creative processes. It is critical to note that all approaches to creativity represent structure. All creative processes dictate a specific sequence of group activity toward a validated result. It is not an unorganized approach with a hope for a "Eureka" response.

Creativity is a frequently misused and misunderstood term in management. Creativity has a socially accepted definition that seems to imply original discoveries such as those by Alexander Graham Bell, Marconi, Edison, and other truly creative geniuses. In reality, very little pure research into totally new directions is implemented. The breakthroughs that occur are usually extensions of variations of existing data bases. Most management creativity is focused on improving existing products, procedures, and practices. To separate it from the less disciplined creative process, we refer to this focus as innovation.

A major research and development laboratory in the telecommunications industry spends ninety percent of its research funds on "mission-oriented research." This is research aimed at achieving specific results on prespecified products or systems. Only ten percent is spent on nondirected research. Thus, innovation is favored nine to one over creativity. The results are such that this lab is recognized worldwide as being one of the foremost in its field. Managers are similarly mission-oriented and thus need innovation processes that lead them to specific results. Although the form of the solution may be totally unspecified, the goal must be clearly defined. Managers are most often in a situation where they must come up with better and different ways of resolving problems or achieving results, This is best accomplished through innovation rather than unbridled creativity. Before describing several techniques for assisting the manager there are several overall principles that should be explored in innovation.

Rational Process	Creative/Innovative Process
Starting Point	
• A problem or need to resolve a situation	• A problem or need to resolve a situation
Problem Statement	
• Usually very specific	• Can be more general in some techniques
Process	
• Requires trained group members	• Requires trained group members
• Basic approach is logical	• Many different approaches— synthesis, brainstorming, morphology, etc.
Aids	
• Visibility via flip charts or easels is important	• Visibility of process is important
Results	
• Normally one "best" choice or solution	• Several possible solutions or none at all
Group roles	
• Members should be there for a purpose: i.e., problem ownership, data source, etc.	• People need not know or own the problem
Input	
• Dependent on validity of data	• Dependent on imagination and creativity of members.

Figure 2.22   Comparison of the Rational and Creative/Innovative Processes.

PRINCIPLE I.   ESTABLISH AN INNOVATIVE CLIMATE

Much has been written about the difficulties of operating in a creative group situation. Theorists have developed detailed lists of perceptual blocks, cultural blocks, and emotional blocks that exist in groups and individuals who restrict the full use of their innovative skills. Thus, it is imperative to consciously establish a climate that allows mistakes, illogic, diversions, unsupported ideas, and other normally undesired group behavior. Without a set of ground rules that encourage freedom (within the structure), innovation will not flourish. Of all the principles in innovation this one is paramount. Without the freedom and the proper climate, no tool will be effective. In most innovation training programs a tremendous amount of time is spent teaching the skills of climate setting.

PRINCIPLE II.   START WITH EASY AND AVAILABLE ALTERNATIVES

In most problem-solving situations, we are not "reworking the world." At best, we are trying to make a modest improvement or correction. First of all, one should consider known solutions that have worked before or are in use in other parts of the organization. Sometimes it is simpler to stand on a chair to change a light-bulb than it is to design a "folding, multiple-length, ambidextrous bulb replacement device."

PRINCIPLE III.   AVOID A PRELIMINARY SEARCH FOR AN IDEAL

Since most workable solutions usually result in taking the best from several competing solutions, it might be unrealistic to expect an alternative to be perfect at first glance. A favorite device used by people who are dedicated organization obstacles is known as the "it won't work approach." They always find a flaw somewhere in the proposal. Their ambition is to discount the entire credibility of the solution for the sake of a minor point (thus providing them with an individual feeling of accomplishment, but often at the expense of any progress.) When searching for possible solutions, we should have an open, nonjudgmental attitude and not eliminate choices that are not ideal. This elimination will come later, in a more disciplined manner, when we compare alternatives.

PRINCIPLE IV. USE OTHER PEOPLE

Encourage others to help you generate a wide range of alternatives. Although a group may not always be the most effective forum for problem solving, it can be effective in creating a wide range of solutions. Synergy, in the form of building on others' ideas or reacting to the inputs of others, can provide a more creative and, perhaps, more useful solution than any single individual could produce. Because individuals tend to limit themselves to single tracks and single definitions, groups' suggestions can be helpful.

For example, when completing a cross-word puzzle, if you attach an interpretation to a clue word too quickly, you may never get the answer. If the word "desert" were a clue, several possible directions could be taken. If you focus on such responses as "Gobi," "Sahara," and the author meant "desert" as in A.W.O.L., or leaving, you may have difficulty in solving the puzzle. However, if another person looks over your shoulder, he or she frequently can point and say, "That's easy," and give you an answer you never would have considered because of your restricted focus. The use of groups provides a fresh viewpoint on the situation, and tends to enhance the objectivity of the alternatives.

Criterion Optimization Technique (COT)

This process-oriented technique can be used to explore variations or alternatives. This normally is applied when none of the known alternatives seems to be appropriate. A fundamental principle of COT is that combinations of the best features of known alternatives can lead to a more effective solution. This process is one that The Alamo Consulting Group has developed to help in situations where traditional alternative generation has not yielded acceptable solutions.

To apply COT the first step is to generate a complete list of desired end results of the decision (criteria). Since the alternatives are not yet going to be evaluated, these are known as Design Criteria. This list of criteria should include the entire range of known desired end results. They represent what we want achieved by the decision. The Design Criteria will form the stimulus for our creative generation of ideas. They provide the direction necessary for productive creativity.

The second step is to take each criterion in turn and optimize an ideal solution to that single factor. All other criteria are pushed out of mind at this point. No alternatives are evaluated at this point. The key question to be used is "What would an alternative that performed perfectly on this criterion look like?" This is repeated for each criterion until a list of optimum alternatives exists.

The process of generating solutions from criteria is where innovation is required. Our experience suggests that this is best achieved through some form of brain storming, green lighting, or group creativity. The application of the key principles of Innovation, mentioned earlier in this section, have their application during this step. The free-wheeling development of ideas increases the possibility of generating the components of an ultimately feasible solution.

The range of alternatives in the Optimum Criteria column now should be assessed for a design package that could incorporate several approaches that would not have been visible without using the Criterion Optimization Technique. Combinations of the best features of known alternatives can lead to a more effective solution.

The first task in combining the Optimum Criteria into a comprehensive alternative is to test for mutual exclusivity. Because each Optimum Criterion has been generated independently, it is conceivable there could be mutually excluding characteristics. Each Optimized Solution is then combined with every other Optimized Solution to check for potential contradictions. Judgment is required at this stage. If two criteria are contradicting, then a conscious choice must be made regarding which one to include in the initial combination.

The next task is to compare each Optimized Solultion for mutual support. There may be natural combinations that will reinforce each other. These should be immediately connected as the basis for a feasible alternative.

The end result sought is a combination of ideas that produce an innovative, "synergistic" alternative.

It may also be possible to put together different combinations of

Optimized Solutions to create more than one alternative. Solutions that evolve out of different combinations can exist independently of each other and provide a basis for a relative choice.

If more than one alternative is created by using the Criterion Optimization Technique, then the decision maker should return to Step Five of the Standard Decision Making Process and compare alternatives. When only one alternative comes from the use of COT the initial design criteria becomes the basis for evaluation.

It is now critical to apply the absolute scoring/weighing process (as described in Multi-Alternative Decision Making) to the newly created alternative to ensure a guaranteed minimal performance level. This protects the decision maker from compromising to the point of ineffectiveness.

To illustrate the application of COT in a simple situation the following example is presented. The example involves an assignment with a client that required the development of a new supervisory development program for new facilities.

COT Example

Decision Purpose: To design a training program for twenty new supervisors for a new plant to be opened in three months.

Design Criteria:

1. Training to be complete within two months.
2. Training time not to exceed ten days.
3. Cost not more than $500/new supervisor.
4. Produce equal quality supervision as at current plant.
5. Produce supervisors capable of carrying out on-the-job training.

For the purposes of this example we can stop our list at this point. Obviously there is a range of other criteria.

Each criterion is now explored as if it were the only factor to be satisfied and the question is asked, "What would an ideal alternative on this specific criterion look like?" Some possible results are shown in Figure 2.23.

The ideas in the Ideas column represent a freely developed list of solutions that emanated from each individual criterion. They were created by a group of people who were consciously attempting to create ideas without judgment or evaluation. The conversion of these randomly generated ideas into a design package that maximizes the benefits of each is the next step. In our example, we found that several ideas were not feasible and were dropped. For example, programmed instruction was eliminated because it was not feasible in the two-month time frame. Other ideas were explored and tested for mutual exclusivity or support. The result was to explore a solution that incorporated many of the individual ideas into a supervisory training package.

CRITERIA OPTIMIZATION TECHNIQUE WORKSHEET

STEP 1. State Decision Purpose

STEP 2. Generate Design Criteria		STEP 3. Develop Optimized Criteria (ideas)
1. Training to be complete within 2 months	Value	a. No training at all required; use current supervisors
2. Training time not to exceed 10 days		a. Use programmed instruction techniques to reduce classroom time b. Spread 10 days into actual job activities to increase productivity
3. Cost not more than $500/ new supervisor		a. Explore government grants for training b. Use rework during training to achieve dollar savings; use own people
4. Produce equal quality supervision as at current mill		a. Transfer a number of current supervisors b. Have new supervisors work in old mill for one month
5. Produce supervisors capable of carrying out on-the-job training		a. Transfer trainers on job assignment as supervisors for six months
Total Value Ideal Score (total value x 10) Minimum Score		

Figure 2.23 Example of developing Optimized Criteria from Design Criteria.

The range of alternatives in the Criterion Optimization column should now be assessed for a design package that would incorporate a whole range of different approaches that would not have been visible without COT.

The ultimate choice in this situation involved a series of actions which included:

Reassignment of a staff trainer as a line supervisor in the new plant for six months with a specific role of working in on-the-job training.

Transfer of eight supervisors from the current plant to provide a minimal level of performance. These supervisors were trained in instructional techniques and trained the remaining new supervisors under a job training program funded by the federal government.

Most effective Decision Making attempts to provide a choice from as wide a range of alternatives as possible. However, as has been illustrated, managers are occasionally faced with situations where innovation is necessary. When these kinds of decisions come up the COT process will allow managers to effectively design alternatives for choice and ultimate implementation.

A flow chart (Figure (2.24) and worksheet (Figure 2.25) provide additional reference to this Decision Making Process.

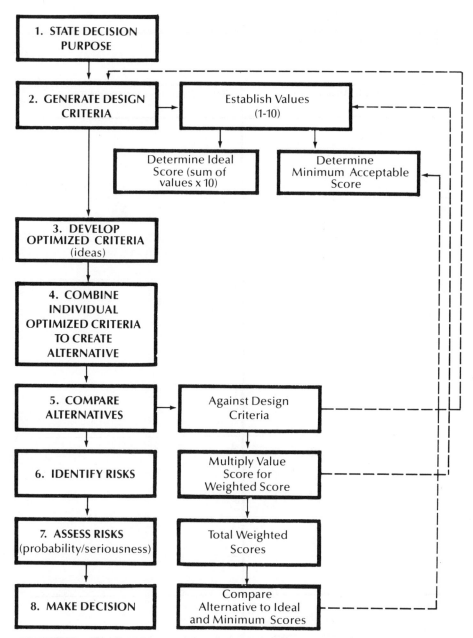

Figure 2.24 Flowchart demonstrating the steps in the Criterion Optimization Technique.

117

CRITERIA OPTIMIZATION TECHNIQUE WORKSHEET

STEP 1. State Decision Purpose

STEP 2. Generate Design Criteria	Value	STEP 3. Develop Optimized Criteria (ideas)
1.		a.
		b.
		c.
2.		a.
		b.
		c.
3.		a.
		b.
		c.
4.		a.
		b.
		c.
5.		a.
		b.
		c.
6.		a.
		b.
		c.
Total Value **Ideal Score (total value x 10)** **Minimum Score**		

Figure 2.25   Worksheet outlining the steps

STEP 4. Combine Individual Criteria to Create Alternative	**STEP 5.** Compare Alternative to Ideal and Minimum Score	Score/ Wt. score

STEP 6. and 7. Identify and Assess Risk (note probability and seriousness)

Alternative	**P / S**
• If:	
• Then:	
• If:	
• Then:	

in the Criterion Optimization Process.

CHAPTER 3

Plan Analysis—The Key to Proactivity

Nothing happens unless the manager makes it happen! Making a decision and selecting a course of action remove uncertainty of one sort, only to replace it with another. Now, the concern of a manager is not, "Which way to go?" but rather, "How do I make it work?" The focus of attention has switched from the present to the future. Effective planning is a means of projecting experience into the future and increasing the effectiveness of a plan. Experience is useful to managers as a means of developing theories of cause when things aren't going well and we have seen that it is also useful in decision making. However, a manager's experience pays off most when a problem is avoided because experience was applied to the effective implementation of a plan. *The most effective manager is proactive rather than reactive.*

Truly effective managers should avoid becoming better and better firefighters. While it is beneficial to continually sharpen our cause analysis skills (if we are myopic) we also run the risk of becoming solely "better reactors." No matter how good a firefighter they are, managers have more impact if that fire is prevented in the first place. This anticipating of problems or side-effects based on experience is fundamental, and yet it seems to receive the least amount of managerial attention. Rewards seem to be given to those high profile managers, who are always pulling off some managerial "slight of hand" to resolve a crisis. They are rewarded as firefighters and not as managers.

No one can absolutely control future events. We can, however, attempt to supplement our plans with some process or structured analysis based on our experience. For example, consider a crisis that occurs in a particular organization from time to time. Mentally list some of those crises. If you deduct all the crises that never have happened in that company you have not made a very big dent in the list. This shows that we often are simply getting better at resolving the same old crises.

The future is made up of two parts, the foreseeable and the unforeseeable. In this chapter, we concentrate on the foreseeable, because we can usually deal with those events of time. However, we will show how to be prepared for the unforeseeable events which are inevitable.

An illustration of this principle might help: A major oil company was required to move an offshore drilling rig from the Indian Ocean to the North Sea. This was going to be either a dream or a nightmare, depending on the engineer's level of management skill. It involved a complex plan including having a fleet of tugs move a huge rig around the Cape of Good Hope and up the coast to the North Sea. There were some absolutely fantastic adventures before the job was complete.

It became a daily, in-company saga to find out what would go wrong next. Every time something did go wrong, it touched off a sea of cables, static, and panic—as well as other irrational responses to uncertainty. When the project was complete, the whole saga was documented and the various problems encountered were listed. The training divison of the company decided to use this project as a learning exercise for developing other managers. They based a training module on these documented facts and formed groups of people who did not know the details of the saga. These "trainees" were managers from finance, administration, marketing, and exploration from many different countries. The groups were given the basic plan for moving the oil rig. Then they were asked to list all the potential problems they considered worth worrying about. On the average, over fifty percent of all the problems that did happen were identified by these groups. In other words, at least half of the problems were foreseeable. Had anybody actually consciously reviewed the original plan to assess the possibility of adverse effects?

The Plan Analysis Process has two basic purposes:

1. To anticipate potential problems so that action can be taken to reduce the possibility of the adverse effects of those problems, answering the question "What could go wrong when this plan is implemented?"
2. To anticipate potential opportunities so that action can be taken to increase the probability and impact of those opportunities, answering the question "What element could go better than expected when this plan is implemented?"

The steps of the Plan Analysis Process follow:

1. State the plan briefly—include end result desired.
2. List/review steps in plan and select critical areas.

3. Identify potential problems/opportunities.
4. Determine likely causes of key potential problems/opportunities.
5. Develop preventive/facilitative action(s).
6. Plan contingent action(s).
7. Build in alarm(s) to trigger contingent action(s).

Step One.   State the Plan Briefly

Describe the plan in one or two sentences. Make certain to include the desired end result of the plan.

Step Two.   Review Steps in Plan and Select Impact Areas

The decision has been made. But nothing happens until someone says, "How do we do it?" A plan can be anything from a mental checklist to a complex, multifunctional, critical path diagram. No matter how complex or simple, all plans are alike in one respect. They represent the activities that must be carried out to get a specified end result. The purpose of this chapter is to teach the skills required to implement plans successfully, to provide a tool for the analysis of the planning function, whether performed individually or with others. This chapter is not intended to be a complete study of the planning function.

All managers' experience should provide them with the content for plans. To assure a level of common understanding, let us establish some guidelines for a plan. A plan, no matter how simple or complex, must minimally contain three elements: (1) a specific list of activities in chronological order, "What must happen?" (2) assigned responsibility, "Who is going to do it?" and (3) a target, "When is it going to be done?"

A manager reviews a plan and selects those parts of the plan that require further attention. That attention might be motivated by several factors, such as:

1. A history of problems in the area.
2. Severity of impact if something did go wrong.
3. Fear of the unknown.
4. Potential payoff if that area could be improved.

In reviewing and evaluating the work of others who have made up an original plan, managers might select two or three parts of the plan for analysis. In effect, they are saying, "If I haven't got time to analyze everything, what would best use my time?" In instances where this approach is used by N.A.S.A. for space launches, every step in the plan is critical. They cannot select only some areas for analysis. They must have

100% success of 100% of the plan. For most managers, however, this depth of planning is unnecessary.

A short illustration might help clarify the Plan Analysis Process and be useful as a vehicle for demonstrating each step. For simplicity, consider the example shown in Figure 3.1.

In this simplified plan, we have indicated that only two parts of the plan really require further analysis. The rest is fairly straightforward; we have done it many times in the past. Our focus now is two impact, or critical, areas. While other steps need just normal attention, these have abnormal analysis requirements. This illustration will be extended at the end of the chapter to illustrate the complete Plan Analysis Process.

Step Three.   *Identify Potential Problems/Opportunities*

This is the stage in the process where experience begins to pay. Here we begin to project that experience to increase the probability of achieving the desired results. If we continue to focus on the cause/effect relationship from the earlier processes, we now need to identify the potential effects that can occur. Effects can be only one of three types: (1) worse than expected (negative deviation), (2) better than expected (positive deviation), or (3) what was expected (norm, or standard).

To carry out this step in the process, we again ask two basic questions. The first is to identify threats or adverse possible effects. The second is to identify opportunities.

Question No. 1   *What could be wrong in this area of the plan? (What has happened in the past? What problems can be foreseen?)*

Planning Statement: Move Purchasing Department into new office location.

STEP 1. List/Review Steps in Plan and Indicate Critical Areas

	Date	By Whom	Critical Areas
1. Arrange for phone installation	3/25	P.A.C.	
2. Notify vendors of new location/phone number	4/1	J.A.G.	
3. Designate new offices to members of Purchasing Staff	4/10	J.A.G.	Can be sensitive area
4. Move Purchasing records/ files and equipment to new location	4/15	P.A.C.	Could have high impact if done well/poorly

Figure 3.1   Outline of a plan for an office move.

The answer to this question is always expressed in terms of the effect, not the cause. This allows for a more positive approach in plan analysis. If potential problems are expressed in terms of cause, there is a danger of only building actions around those causes.

Question No. 2. *What payoffs could occur if a critical area went better than expected? (What pleasant surprises have occurred in the past? For example, if a responsibility was completed before a deadline, how could the extra time be used?)*

This question tries to build positively toward the Plan Analysis Process. Many opportunities are missed because we aren't ready to take advantage of them. "If only I had known!"

Together these questions will yield a list of potential problems and opportunities. However, both cannot be done simultaneously. Better results occur when they are listed separately—even if the method is similar. In practice, we recommend that managers fully complete potential problem analysis and then recycle through opportunity analysis. One of the creative steps in the process, this is a useful place to utilize the experience of others. Sometimes others see threats or opportunities that we fail to identify because we are too close to the situation.

ASSESS PROBLEMS/OPPORTUNITIES FOR PROBABILITY AND SERIOUSNESS/BENEFITS

Before we "gnash our teeth" and "break into tears" about this long list of potential problems and opportunities, it makes sense to temper our analysis with a little judgement about priority. There is no need or time for a manager to react to every potential problem or opportunity. We should worry about the "big ones." "Big," in terms of predictive measurement, was covered in the Risk Analysis portion of Decision Making. As stated in the chapter on Decision Making, there are two dimensions to Risk Assessment: Probability and Serioussness.   Using managerial judgement, review the list of potential problems and indicate high/medium/low (in terms of probability of that effect occurring), and then the impact (seriousness), of its occurrence. In looking at opportunities, indicate the probability of the opportunity arising and the benefit of its occurrence.

Step Four.   Determine Likely Causes of Key Potential Problems/Opportunities

It shouldn't be surprising that the next step in the process is to seek out the Likely Causes of these high risk potential effects. The purpose of this step is to focus on proaction, rather than reaction. If we can isolate some of the likely causes of our potential effects, it is easier to plan actions to manage those effects.

To illustrate this concept, consider a quick example.

If managers were told, "Fire control is your responsibility and you should do something about it," it would not be easy to direct their efforts. They might be prone to take any and all actions which might have a bearing on the situation. If, on the other hand, someone said, "There are four highly probable causes of fire in your current operation and I want them corrected," it would not be difficult to act quickly and with direction against the causes. If we take the time to predict effect, we similarly should take the time to predict likely causes.

The source of anticipating likely cause is experience: for example, "If increased overtime caused problems in the past, it has a good chance of doing the same again." This is another phase of process enhanced from the inputs of others. Sometimes we can only see potential causes external to ourselves. Other people often bring an objectivity that can increase our range of likely causes.

To carry out this step, simply take each identified potential problem and opportunity and ask the question: "What could cause this effect?" The causes then are listed for use in planning further action. Figure 3.2 should

PLAN ANALYSIS WORKSHEET

STEP 1. State the Plan Briefly (end result desired): Move Purchasing Department into New Office Location

STEP 2. List/Review Steps in Plan and Indicate Critical Areas			STEP 3. Identify Potential Problems/Opportunities (probability and seriousness of priorities)		STEP 4. Determine Likely Causes of Key Potential Problems/Opportunities
• Designate new offices to members of purchase staff	Date	By Whom	• Friction and conflict among staff members over office designation (potential problem)	P / S	• Staff members see method of designation as inequitable (favoritism is suspect)
• Move purchasing records/files and equipment to new location			• Opportunity to revise record keeping/filing system (potential opportunity)		• People have to involve themselves with the whole system to move. The size and utility of the system will come under scrutiny

Figure 3.2   The first three steps in Plan Analysis using the office moving example.

clarify this concept. It is critical to develop a list of likely causes rather than to generate a single cause and build protection against that isolated cause.

Step Five.   Develop Preventive/Facilitative Action(s)

It is only common sense to do something about something that could help or hurt us. Few off us like to be totally powerless in the face of life's vicissitudes. In this step, managers should be proactive by doing something about the potential effects to influence the future.

Having predicted that something is going to happen, and having predicted what one thinks will cause it to happen, we must now focus our actions on these predictions. There are two types of action possible. One type deals with cause and one with effect. A managerial awareness of the types of the various actions adopted goes far in keeping temporary solutions from becoming instituitonalized and continuing after the "problem" has gone away.

If we state that a certain cause might produce a certain effect, we need to explore what action, if any, should be directed toward that cause. If the effect is adverse or negative (potential problem), then the action should be aimed at reducing the likelihood of that cause occurring. This we call Preventive Action. If, however, the potential is positive, we want to increase the probability of that effect's occurring. The appropriate action in this event is called Facilitative Action. Preventive and Facilitative Actions are added to our original plan. They become incorporated into our plan as integral steps. Conscious consideration of what can be done without doing it is useless. This is a key step in adding to the degree of control we have over achieving results. The feeling of powerlessness is attacked by active inclusion of actions that affect the probability.

Step Six.   Plan Contingent Action(s)

In Preventive Actions we attempt to manipulate probability. However, the problem still has a potential for occurring. One can never guarantee the elimination of a potential problem. For this reason, effective managers usually develop Contingent Actions to alleviate or minimize their effects, if they do occur. If something goes wrong, a manager may react by considering, "What do I do now?" or "It's time to move into action . . . Plan B." Most managers would like to have the capability of moving into a previously developed standby or contingent position.

If the effect we are protecting against is sufficient to be worth managing, we need to develop a Contingent Action. This action answers the question, "If this problem arises, what will I do?" Contingent Actions against negative effects are normally disruptive, costly, and undesirable. Managers would like never to use their contingencies. The use of the Contingency Action means the problem has occurred. Department stores have sprinkler systems and hope they never have to be used; we buy fire insurance and hope we never have to use it. These are examples of contingencies.

A contingency is by definition a second-best action. It is a safety release that is deemed essential and yet should be avoided until absolutely required. The parachutist does not want to engage the reserve chute until absolutely necessary because it can foul up the main chute if that later deploys. The baseball manager wants to wait until it is absolutely necessary to use a relief pitcher in a ball game.

In the event of positive deviations and opportunities, there is an equal need for Contingent Action. Opportunities must be seized. Even if opportunities are identified and facilitated, they must be acted on. If you have increased the probability of opportunity knocking on your door by means of advertising, you had better make sure that your salesmen are prepared to follow up on new leads.

Many opportunities are lost because the individual has not been in a position to take advantage of the situation. The steps of recognition have occurred; however, exploitation has not been provided for.

Step Seven.   Build in Alarm(s)

An additional consideration must be built into the plan; a mechanism by which the manager can activate the contingency. This must be predetermined; if left to chance the contingency might be ineffective—that is, the opportunity missed or the problem too far advanced. This step is called the Contingency Alarm. It is a predetermined point that tells the planner to activate the contingency. Any contingency that is developed must have an Alarm. Without an Alarm, there is no guarantee about the potential impact or timing of the contingency.

The Alarm is not simply a milepost or a point in time. It is the occurrence or nonoccurrence of certain events at a prescribed time. In baseball the manager's alarm might be "Any two people on base after 120 pitches means bring in the relief pitcher." A manager might indicate that "nonarrival of key raw materials at a specified date" means reallocation of workers to other production lines. Good managers are constantly monitoring plans to permit the planned actions to be as effective as is feasible.

Let's go back to our example about moving the purchasing department (Figure 3.1) and see how this ties together with the other steps in the process. We identified two activities as having potential impact (critical areas): (1) designate new offices to members of purchasing staff and (2) move purchasing records/files and equipment to new location.

In our assessment of impact areas, the first area was seen as a potential troublespot and the second, if handled well, a potential positive area. We can thus illustrate anticipating threat and opportunity. A Plan Analysis worksheet completing Steps Four through Six might look like Figure 3.3.

These are examples of how an analytical plan can put us into a position of preventing the occurrence of threats and being ready to take advantage of opportunities. An opportunity that is missed can be as serious to us as the problems we attempt to prevent.

The process of successful Plan Analysis represents an attempt to make things happen by projecting our experience into the future. If we ignore the threats of potential problems or fail to anticipate opportunities, we are not being as effective as we could be. The key to success is to focus one's thinking on the one or two critical impact areas, and look at those areas for threats or opportunities and likely cause. It is then possible to outline the appropriate actions necessary to successfully implement the plan.

A flow chart (Figure 3.4) and blank worksheet (Figure 3.5) are provided for further reference. A case study, Velex Laboratories, and practical applications are also included here.

PLAN ANALYSIS WORKSHEET

STEP 5. Develop Preventive/Facilitative Action	STEP 6. Plan Contingent Action(s)	STEP 7. Build in Alarms to Trigger Contingent Action(s)
Preventive Action • Conduct random designation of office space and make method visible (preventive)	• Publish memo offering to discuss any unhappiness with new office space and attempt to accomodate reasonable considerations	• When 3 or more complaints have been reported by key supervisor or others
Facilitative Action • Hold staff meeting outlining opportunities with current filing/records system (facilitative)	• Have a preliminary meeting with methods people to have a systems analyst available to design and implement new system	• When 3 or more ideas are generated about developing new system

Figure 3.3 Steps Four through Six in Plan Analysis using the office moving example.

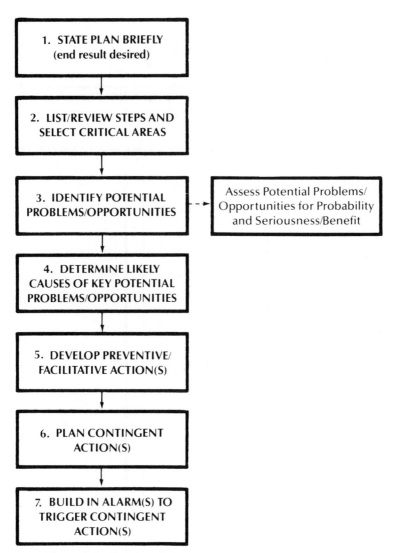

Figure 3.4   Flowchart demonstrating the Plan Analysis Process.

PLAN ANALYSIS WORKSHEET

STEP 1. State the Plan Briefly (end result desired)

STEP 2. List/Review Steps in Plan and Indicate Critical Areas			STEP 3. Identify Potential Problems/Opportunities (probability and seriousness of priorities)		STEP 4. Determine Likely Causes of Key Potential Problems/Opportunities
	Date	By Whom		P/S	

Figure 3.5 Worksheet outlining

STEP 5. Develop Preventive/Facilitative Action(s)	STEP 6. Plan Contingent Action(s)	STEP 7. Build In Alarms to Trigger Contingent Action(s)

the Plan Analysis Process.

VELEX LABORATORIES

Velex Laboratories is a widely successful international organization specializing in health and medical products which has recently extended its geographical dominion by adding two overseas plants and one domestic operation in the past two years. The commitment to research and development at Velex is also increasing, and in an effort to expand product lines they are anxious to create a new division of Nutritional Supplements. Research done by the marketing division has shown this to be a potentially highly profitable market, especially on the west coast.

Velex's president and chief executive officer, J.R. Bradley, is actively seeking a top person to head this new company division. While he holds firmly to the principle of hiring on the basis of qualifications and job-related ability, he is also very aware of the affirmative action guidelines recently set up by the federal government. There are several people among his present business contacts whom he feels might be considered qualified applicants, but he is aware that those contacts are limited and feels that it will be necessary to recruit from other areas if he is to achieve his goals.

With this in mind, Bradley decided to send his vice-president, Tom Southern to a conference in New Orleans entitled "Modern Medicine: Too Much Dope?" Bradley chose this particular conference because he realized that the field of holistic medicine is rapidly gaining both credence and popularity among the public, and someone who is familiar with this area of health care would be an asset for a division dealing with nutritional supplements. Tom Southern, also interested in holistic health approaches, readily accepted the assignment. His job was two-fold: to take note of the research and developments in this particular approach to medicine, and to bring back a qualified division head for Velex's new operation. Since approximately 5000 people were expected to attend the conference, Southern felt confident that he would be able to accomplish his task.

Arriving in New Orleans the evening before the conference sessions began, Southern took time to review the upcoming program. He noted with special interest a paper to be given on "The Effects of Megavitamin Therapy on Four Common Killer Diseases: Cancer, Heart Disease, Diabetes, and Stroke." Having been an insulin-dependent diabetic himself for the last ten years, Southern put this particular presentation at the top of his list.

132

The next afternoon Southern found himself in a large meeting room with approximately 150 people. Seated behind a table and podium at the front of the room was Don Cameron, the man who was to deliver the paper on Megavitamin Therapy. Cameron spoke very well, referring only occasionally to the notes in front of him, and seemed comfortable both with his topic and with the role of public speaker. The subject matter was fascinating, and, after listening with rapt attention to the amazing effects of nondrug therapy, Southern was convinced that this was the man needed to do the job at Velex. He saw in Cameron an intelligent, confident man who spoke clearly in terms that even lay people could comprehend, and noticed that he was well-received by his audience and accorded the respect of an expert in his field.

Southern was curious, though, about how Cameron would handle the question-and-answer period that was to follow, since this would not be prepared but extemporaneous material. Cameron fielded the questions very well, coming directly to the point and speaking to the issue. But the vice-president noticed something else: Often Cameron would turn to a man seated at the table next to him and have the question repeated before he answered. The questions that needed repetition were those that originated in the back of the room, but were as audible as those which came from the audience in the front. It suddenly became clear to Southern that Cameron had a hearing loss, and could answer unassisted only those questions from the front of the room where the volume was sufficiently loud.

Southern still wanted to set up an appointment with Don Cameron during the conference to discuss the position at Velex. As he made his way to the front of the room he saw Don leave the table. He had not been aware that Cameron was in a wheelchair.

Many thoughts ran through Southern's mind at that point. "He's an excellent researcher, very knowledgeable in his field. He's well-received by his audience and respected by his peers. But he is, well—handicapped." By that time the vice-president had reached the front of the room, and, putting his doubts aside, he arranged a meeting with Cameron for later that evening.

The vice-president's interview with Don was very favorable. Don had just the experience the company needed; his extensive background in nutritional research and development could put Velex way out in front of its competitors. The vice-president was ready to hire him—any problems would have to be worked out as things went along.

Several calls were placed to Velex's President. Bradley was surprised and somewhat apprehensive about the situation and had no ready answers as to how some of the problems would be handled. But he trusted Southern's judgement and realized the importance of having the new division headed by a person with Cameron's qualifications and reputation. He told Southern to hire Don Cameron.

Cameron had received several offers from people attending the convention, and after due consideration decided he would join the Velex organization as head of the new division in one month's time.

How could plans to introduce and orient Don Cameron to Velex Laboratories be successfully implemented? An outline of the planned first day's activities is attached.

INTRODUCTION AND ORIENTATION TO VELEX LABORATORIES

Don Cameron, New Director

Nutritional Supplements Division

Monday, May 15

9:00 A.M.	Meet professional staff and other division directors (Room 103).
10:30 A.M.	Visit laboratory research areas (basement)—Meet technicians, examine equipment.
11:30 A.M.	Meet support staff (Room 110)
12:00 Noon	Lunch with J. R. Bradley, Velex President (Perkins Steak House) 3 miles East of Velex on State Hwy 88.
2:00 P.M.	Visit personnel office (Room 204)—Complete necessary forms, review employee manual.
3:30 P.M.	Report to office area (Room 116)—Look over office furniture, equipment, supplies.

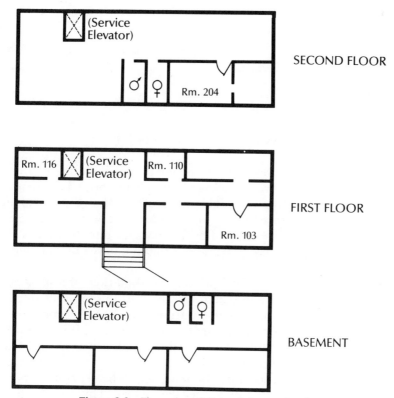

Figure 3.6   Floor plan of Velex Laboratories, Inc.

COMPUTER SOFTWARE IMPLEMENTATION

A medium-sized computer software company was installing its first pilot facility with a new software package. The client was a key user of the software company's programs. This particular software implementation was to be the first of three major installations. The software design team had advanced to the stage of installing the package into the client's system. All of the debugging, redesign, and program development had been completed.

The project team held a final meeting on the Friday morning prior to the Monday launch date at the client's location. At this meeting, the project team invited the key liaison person from the client organization. The purpose of the meeting was to ensure that the plan for software installation went according to schedule. The meeting produced two key Potential Problems that had been overlooked.

Daily feedback to the software company was to be generated at the end of each working day via a data package return. This would allow the software company to be aware of daily results and problems. Because of the two hour time difference between the client company and the software company, this transmission would create two difficulties. Primarily, it would be received after working hours in the software house and thus require overtime and additional staff to review and react. Second, the key data transmission usage of the data network was highest during this period. Concern was expressed about the ability to consistently log in and get a data line from the client to the software company. The line being used was a nondedicated line.

Because of these projected difficulties, it was possible to modify the plan to have the installation team send their daily reports at 7:00 a.m. at the client location and be received at 9:00 a.m. at the software company. This was a low-usage period on the data network and also provided the installation team extra time to attempt on-site modifications prior to sending the data.

The result was several on-site program modifications that were worked out overnight and saved many dollars and hours that would have been spent at the company headquarters. It also provided an extra sense of responsibility and achievement for the installation team.

PERFORMANCE APPRAISAL LAUNCH

A major telecommunications company in Canada had developed a comprehensive new performance appraisal program for its professional and management personnel. The design and process was complete and the manpower planning group developed a plan to launch the new process.

Prior to launching the new process, the group did a preliminary analysis of its plan for opportunities and potential problems. They invited two key line managers and an outside consultant to assist in the generation of the potential effects. In a half-hour the group identified three key potential problems and one major opportunity.

Potential Problems

1. The launch date for the program would conflict with year-end budget consolidation and wrap-up.
2. The plan omitted the inclusion of branch plants that were already feeling ignored by corporate headquarters.
3. The translation into French to meet legal requirements was underestimated in terms of the time estimates.

Potential Opportunity

1. The personnel department had just completed a managers' manual for personnel issues, and these two programs might serve as mutually supporting launch vehicles.

As a result of the analysis, there were several Facilitative Actions taken. Primarily, the program was delayed until January, as opposed to December. This avoided the conflict with budget consolidation and allowed the French translation to be completed.

New launch sessions were added to include branch facilities to ensure that all managers would be covered. The two programs, Personnel Manual and Performance Appraisal, were combined and the result was a stronger launch and less time loss on the part of line managers.

Plan Analysis is a process of avoiding foreseeable difficulties and increasing the probability of success. The use of managers from other departments can provide insights that may not be apparent within the planning group.

CHAPTER 4

Situation Review

So far, we have discussed how managers can react when the nature of uncertainty is clear and singular. In Cause Analysis, there is a need to find cause to arrive at an effective solution to a problem. In Decision Making, there is a need to choose a best course of action or select an alternative. In Plan Analysis, there is a need to be proactive in order to insure the successful implementation of our decisions. Unfortunately, situations don't come to a manager's desk with color-coded ribbons and little notes that read, "I'm a problem to be solved," "A decision to be made," "A plan to be implemented." When concerns are this clear the reaction is quite simple. Identify your appropriate analytical thought process (Cause Analysis/Decision Making/Plan Analysis) and go to work.

Most often, the situations presented to us are not singular. On any given day at the office there is more than one thing to do. For these situations, managers need some method of concern appraisal. They need some means of sorting out, evaluating priority, and getting started. This process we call Situation Review. The other thought processes we have looked at have a sequential set of steps leading to a predetermined endpoint, for example, cause-choice-implementation. The endpoint of Situation Review is to have arranged what needs to be done in a form that helps you attack the right concerns, in the right order, with the right technique, for the right reasons.

There are four basic steps in the process:

1. Identify and list concerns (and effects that require management).
2. Separate/clarify concerns (if necessary).
3. Establish priorities (impact, urgency, and trends).
4. Determine the starting point for analysis.

Step One. Identify and List Concerns

All of our processes begin with a reference to cause/effect. Situation Review is no different. As managers, we are continually managing effects. We are constantly reacting to undesirable effects, trying to create effects through decisions, or protecting against and optimizing effects in plan implementation. It is for this reason that we begin our process by reviewing managerial responsibility areas for situational effects that require action and attention.

There are two words that need to be defined for our consideration of Situation Review.

Situation
A situation is an event, a happening; it is time-based. It is a description of what's happening. An example would be a memo from your boss which includes a reference to a large, new order. It happens and is reported. Nothing is done with it.

Concern
A concern is very different. It is a description of a manager's need to take action on, or pay attention to, a particular situation. In our example of the large, new order, some managers would treat it as a situation, be aware of it, and retain the information. Other managers would identify it as a concern because, for them, it is a need to plan production schedules, order materials, check machine loadings and maintenance schedules, and so on. Thus, managers convert a situation to a concern by identifying their own need to act. They seek the effect, or potential effect, of that situation on their responsibility.

Managers manage concerns and effects. This process of determining concerns is very much dependent on a constant review of the various situations we face. A manager who doesn't know what's happening will not be able to anticipate the need for action. Good managers have highly developed information sensing systems which allow them to be proactive and identify concerns long before they become visible in the form of "crises." These information systems are very much tied to the establishment of goals or objectives. Writers in the field of management by objectives agree that the establishment of clear objectives within a manager's area of responsibility permits more rapid and consistent identification of concerns.

There are several applications where listing concerns can be helpful. One instance would be the staff meeting. The purpose is to review progress on a range of concerns and determine actions required. The listing of concerns/effects as a first step can be very useful as a means of saving time. There is a frequent tendency to try to resolve every issue as it arises at a meeting. A systematic listing gives a manager the capability of not only assessing the entirety of the concerns, but of attaching and assigning responsibility for later attention.

A second instance is in the planning of a fixed time frame. Managers trying to plan the use of their time for a day or a week should first list all the effects that require their attention. Priority, as we shall see, is a relative process and only if the list is complete can proper time allocation be made.

A cautionary note in listing concerns: Avoid items such as "review," "discuss," and "investigate." These describe the activity, not the effect a manager is trying to manage. It is much more useful to state the concern in terms of the effect. A manager does not really wish to "review progress on a new product launch," but, rather, to "determine any actions required to keep new product launch on schedule." This is a more proactive approach.

Step Two.   Separate/Clarify Concerns (if necessary)

This step may not be essential in all situations. Frequently, a concern or effect is clear and singular. Only one action or one cause identification will be required. In such instances, there is no need to separate, move on to the next stage, establishing priority. Examples of these singular concerns might be as follows:

High scrap rate from #13 Extruder (a clear-cut need for Cause Analysis). Select a new secretary for purchasing office (a clear-cut need for Decision Making).

There will, however, be times when there is a lot of confusion over the exact nature of the concern. This often occurs when things are stated in general terms, for example, "We have a morale problem," "We have communications difficulties." Such generalized statements are impossible to manage effectively.

There might also be confusion because there are several concerns introduced in the statement of concern, for example, "We need to decide on the marketing plan, price structure, and packaging details for our new product." This is more than one concern and cannot be treated as a single, manageable effect. It is in reaction to concerns like these that a manager needs to break the effects apart so that they may be analyzed individually. A key question to determine if separation is required is, "Will one action or cause explain or resolve this situation?" If the response to this question is no, then separation is required.

If we identify a need to break a concern into smaller parts, there should be a means for doing this. The process is, of course, the use of questions. The questions are the key to separation.

First Question:

"What kind of concern am I dealing with?"

a. A general description (i.e., morale, people, quality control problems).

b. A collection of seemingly related effects (turnover is too high in Quality Control, Finance, and Personnel).

If it is the first type of situation, suffering from over-generalization, then it is appropriate to ask the other types of questions.

Follow-Up Questions:

"What do you mean by 'communication' problems?"

"In what ways do you know you have a 'communication' problem manifesting itself?"

"In what form is the 'communication' problem manifesting itself?"

"What else is wrong?"

These questions attempt to reduce a complex problem into its component parts—to isolate the specific effects to be dealt with in a logical manner. The purpose is to make proper analysis possible. Frequently, many of the components require different forms of analysis—Cause Analysis, Decision Making, Plan Analysis. No manager in history has ever solved a morale problem! At least not until it was first reduced to its component parts.

If the concern requiring separation is the second type, the reduction process is a little easier. In this instance, the separate effects are usually included in the statement of the concern. In our example of "The turnover is too high in Quality Control, Finance, and Personnel," separation requires the simple question, "Is it safe to assume that the cause is common?" If not, then each unit must be considered separately. We then have three statements of concern: (1) turnover is too high in Quality Control, (2) turnover is too high in Finance, and (3) turnover is too high in Personnel.

If the concern is decision-oriented, the same process applies except that the question is, "Will one decision satisfy all of these parts?" If not, then each component is listed as a separate decision. In this type of separation the subconcerns all remain in the same stage of the analysis cycle, for example, CA or DM.

In summary, separation is a process of breaking an identified concern into its component parts so we don't waste time trying for the one magic solution that solves all problems at once.

Step Three.   Establish Priorities

Having listed our concerns and assured that they are in a form and level where analysis is possible, we are now ready to take some action. But what action? Which concern should be handled first?In our example of separating the turnover rate, three separate concerns were indicated: (1) high turnover in Quality Control, (2) high turnover in Finance, and (3) high turnover in Personnel.

These must all be analyzed. We need a means of quickly selecting the most important. The difficulty in agreeing on priority lies in the difficulty of defining importance. What's important to one manager may not be important to another. There are may ways to set priority and nothing should be used that replaces the individual manager's judgment. However, some tools may be used to help arrange the facts so that judgment can be brought to bear on them.

A list of typical criteria used for defining importance might include:

Impact/seriousness.
Urgency/timing.
Trend/growth.
Potential payoff.
Resources.
Time estimate for resolution.

Effective managers consider all of these in determining the priority of their actions. For simplicity, we suggest managers take the criteria that they feel are most important and use these as a matrix with the individual concerns. Usually a minimal list of criteria would include: Impact, Urgency, and Trend.

As an example, Figure 4.1 shows how we could list our three concerns and three criteria. A quick ranking of these concerns, based on the facts, would provide a working list of prioritized concerns. In assigning priority, it is important to note three guidelines:

SITUATION REVIEW WORKSHEET

STEP 2. Separate/Clarify Concerns	STEP 3. Establish Priorities			
	Impact	Urgency	Trend	Final Priority
• High turnover rate in quality control • High turnover rate in finance • High turnover rate in personnel				

Figure 4.1 Listing of components of a major personal concern.

1. All rankings are done vertically, comparing the various concerns to one another. They are always based on relative impact, relative urgency, relative trend.

2. The rankings can be equal. There is no reason that two concerns can't be equally serious.

3. All rankings are based on data, not opinion. There should be discussion about why a turnover rate in Quality Control has more impact that it does in Personnel.

If we applied this ranking, we might come up with the type of end result shown in Figure 4.2.

In this example, we have ranked the concerns relative to one another with the most serious receiving a "1" (Quality Control), the second most serious a "2," and so on, completing our priority matrix.

Step Four.   Determine Starting Point for Analysis

Since we started the process of Situation Review because of uncertainty, at this point we would be able to specify our clarified concerns in final statements of effect. This stage is simply the check-step that assures that we apply the appropriate analytical process to each concern. We now ask, for each concern identified, "What do I want to have when I finish my analysis? Do I need to find the cause of an effect, do I want to create a certain effect, or do I want to protect or maximize a plan?"

This step will help the manager determine the proper rational process, and, if warranted, delegate the concern along with the identified rationale and logical process.

In summary, Situation Review is a filter. It is a means of clarifying our uncertainty. Concerns are not resolved in Situation Review. What does

SITUATION REVIEW WORKSHEET

STEP 2. Separate/Clarify Concerns	STEP 3. Establish Priorities			
	Impact	Urgency	Trend	Final Priority
• High turnover rate in quality control	1	2	1	1
• High turnover rate in finance	3	3	2	3
• High turnover rate in personnel	2	1	3	2

Figure 4.2   Establishing priorities of manageable concerns.

happen is that we list our manageable concerns, in order of priority, and classified by desired end result. When other processes do not give satisfactory answer or there are so many things happening that it's difficult to get started, consider backing off and doing a Situation Review.

A flowchart of key steps (Figure 4.3) and a worksheet (Figure 4.4) are provided for further reference. Some practical applications of the Situation Review Process follow.

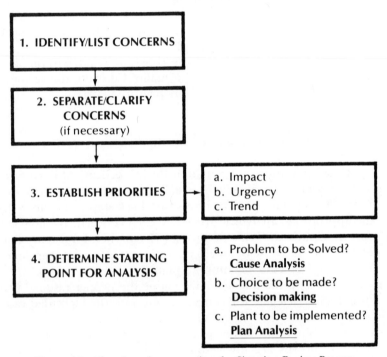

Figure 4.3   Flowchart demonstrating the Situation Review Process.

SITUATION REVIEW WORKSHEET

STEP 1. Identify/List Concerns	STEP 2. Separate/Clarify Concerns (if necessary)	STEP 3. Establish Priorities*				STEP 4. Determine Starting Point for Analysis*
		Impact	Urgency	Trend	Final Priority	

*Data to consider in establishing priorities:

• Impact: Money? Resources? Negative effects?

• Urgency: Whose deadline? Can we do nothing?

• Trend: Increasing? Decreasing? Stable?

*Determine starting point for analysis:

• Problem to be solved? C.A.

• Choice to be made? D.M.

• Plan to be implemented? P.A.

Figure 4.4 Worksheet outlining the Situation Review Process.

145

APPLICATION EXAMPLES

COSTLY DEPARTURES

A major high-technology company conducted a Situation Review that indicated a deep concern about the high turnover rate of professional employees. Upon further separation of the issue, it was found that two areas required consideration: the expensive turnover of new-hires, the most highly recruited graduates with advanced degrees and with the highest grade point averages; and the (also costly) departure of older professionals who had been with the company seven years or longer. A committee was formed to study the issue further and to make a specific recommendation.

Cause Analysis of the first concern showed the two most significant factors to this turnover rate were (1) under-accomplishment in the first year; for example, the employees interviewed felt they were being employed in work that was beneath their level of performance; and (2) lack of challenge or interesting work; the employees interviewed felt that the managers they worked for were incapable of motivating them. With this information, the committee established a decision statement: "What is the best way to retain new technical professional employees for our company?" To identify the Decision Criteria they determined who would be affected by the final outcome of this decision at every level—executive, middle-management, and entry management levels.

In examining their findings and the resources that these people had, the committee prepared a set of criteria they believed best represented the organization's needs and resource limitations. A number of criteria were outlined including, "Do a better job of meeting the employee's objectives." The alternative which best met this criterion was to recruit the employee, determine his or her technical interest, then place that person in a related position in the company. People involved with chip technology would be placed there on the assumption that they would be most motivated in that area. New employees would be given the most challenging work possible and work with the best managers available. The best managers would be those who had the ability to motivate and to sustain motivation over a period of time, and who had the communication skills to work effectively with recent graduates. This alternative was eventually proposed to the management and accepted; the end result was a new policy which was implemented and became a huge success.

A different committee was established within the company to investigate the high turnover among professionals who had been with the company seven years or more. A Cause Analysis identified location among the most significant factors. Most of the company's existing plant, production, and R & D facilities were located in an area on the West Coast where housing costs and the general cost of living were relatively high. Based on the recognition of that situaion, the company decided to begin locating its physical plants in areas where the cost of living was low but the labor force was plentiful. It also would locate as close to qualified technical schools as possible. This decision would move the company's future locations away from the existing plant facilities. Over a three-year period, the company expanded dramatically. Following the policy of locating facilities in sound economic areas, it managed to staff those locations with people who had been with the company for years and were delighted to stay beyond the seventh year.

BAD SAFETY RECORD

A large U.S. paper company was distressed about a bad safety record. This broadly-stated situation was too vague to resolve adequately; therefore, it was separated into its components. The original "bad safety record" was broken down into two separate parts: lost time accidents and doctor's cases. In looking at these concerns, it was discovered that the doctor's cases caused the greater alarm because they involved (1) personal injury requiring treatment by a physician and (2) high cost to the company, increasing its insurance costs and creating poor employee morale.

The doctor's cases from the previous year were reviewed. The statistics from the safety office and the industrial relations office showed that the majority were for abrasions and cuts. These were viewed as just normal events in a rough working environment. The next largest percentage were back injuries. If something could be done to minimize the doctor's cases attributable to lower back strain and muscle spasms, then a large part of the "bad safety problem" could be eliminated.

Having thus separated the doctor's cases and established priorities, the next step was to determine how best to resolve the "lower back injury" issue. The cause of the back injuries was not known. In order to adequately resolve the accident issue, the underlying cause would need to be determined and appropriate preventive measures developed.

Having separated the "bad safety record" into the two major components and identified a top priority (lower back injuries), the company was able to use the relevant process (Cause Analysis) to solve the problem.

ROUTINE STAFF MEETINGS

The department manager of a major electronics firm uses the Situation Review Process to maintain an ongoing assessment of what issues need resolution. The routine staff meetings are used as a means of eliciting and enumerating the issues rather than as a means of resolving them. The department manager has each of her managers give a status report. A composite list is made. The result is that the department manager always has a current list of issues. She knows which items have the highest priority and whose responsibility it is to resolve them. This manager thus puts herself in a position of managing the managers' results rather than their activities.

MARGINALLY PROFITABLE ORGANIZATION

The new president of a cryogenic company had the responsibility to take a marginally profitable organization and turn it around in a very short period of time. His first step involved a series of meetings with top level executives to determine what issues required action, by whom, and when. He used the Situation Review Process to "manage" these meetings. The typical pitfall the president avoided was the tendency to take the issues one at a time and attempt to resolve each one then and there, before finding out what other problems existed.

The president spent a number of days interviewing his executives. The end result was a list of statements representing the health of their business from best case to worst case—past, present, and future. The president sorted these issues into categories.

The next step was to take each of those issues and determine if further separation was required. Once the list had been revised, the president was able to determine the priority of the various issues. He subdivided them into a set of priorities which required immediate, near future, and long range action. Eventually, the priorities were set.

Finally, the president took the highest priority issue and determined whether it was an issue that required Cause Analysis, Decision Making, or Plan Analysis. His top issue was to develop a new marketing plan and an international marketing organization to implement this plan. He determined that the Decision Making Process was the management technique needed.

MANAGEMENT IMPLICATIONS

CHAPTER 5

People Problems

I t is easy to see the benefits of applying a systematic process to problem solving in the manufacturing and systems arenas. In hardware problems, where machines and products don't have feelings or absorb and conceal their reactions to change, a rational approach has proven very effective. But what about the area of People Problems? How can a rational process be applied to people who are not rational, who are, rather, unpredictable, emotional, often changeable, and, more often, very resistant to change? Can we apply the Cause Analysis technique to these People Problems?

The answer is yes—but important distinctions exist. In situations involving people, the ability to manage emotion and to look at facts objectively is perhaps even more critical. Many times these issues are presented in a vague manner, and it is all too easy to introduce feelings into the fact-gathering steps. To guard against these pitfalls, and to help avoid subjectivity, one of the strongest aids is "process questioning" as discussed in the previous chapters of this book.

In the following pages, we look at the specific application of the Cause Analysis Process techniques to People Problems, examine some characteristic difficulties of People Problems, and briefly discuss some basic principles underlying all effective people management techniques.

Although not the complete answer, rational process is an especially needed and valuable tool in sorting out and resolving People Problems.

CHARACTERISTICS OF PEOPLE PROBLEMS

If we define a "People Problem" as a deviation by an individual or a group where the observed behavior or performance is not at the expected level and for which cause is unknown, then the applicability of Cause Analysis is fairly clear.

Before reviewing this application of the process step by step, it is important to be aware of some concepts typical of People Problems.

Unpredictable Reactions

When managers change a business system they are able to anticipate a specific effect, and will expect the same result from the same change every time. When dealing with people and change, however, we know that almost the opposite is true. One change might produce twenty different reactions within a group of twenty people. Learning to anticipate and consider human reaction is an important skill for the proactive manager to develop.

Lack of Quality Data

Human beings don't always say what they mean and the result of this can be vague information about performance problems or behavior. People also have a tendency to interpret rather than simply report what they observe, and it is difficult to check out interpretations factually. For example, a supervisor may report that an employee "has a bad attitude toward his job" when the real behavior causing concern is that the employee is consistently late to work. The manager focusing on an effective questioning technique can become skilled at drawing out facts from interpretations such as this.

Bias and Emotionalism

When a manager hears a sweeping general statement such as "these younger employees don't care about the quality of their work," it is apparent that some personal bias has surfaced. For the manager attempting to deal with people concerns, such statements confuse rather than clarify the issues. In much the same way, human emotions can act to cloud the information regarding an employee problem. Where people are involved, there is a natural tendency to see and hear selectively. Consequently, the manager's job becomes more difficult when managing People Problems. Once again, precise process questioning can be a valuable technique in sorting out fact from emotional release.

Unclear/Unrealistic Expectations

Too often what appears to be a performance problem, requiring much attention, is actually the result of an expectation not being clearly communicated to the employee. It is critical to the success of both manager and employee that expectations and the significance of certain expected performance be clearly expressed and understood. Many times, as soon as the employee understands what is required, the "problem" vanishes. On the other hand, sometimes the expectations are clear and well understood, but totally unrealistic. Goals, standards, and expectations must be reasonable in proportion to the skills and abilities of the employee.

Lack of Feedback

Of all the difficulties in managing people, the area of providing feedback, both positive and negative, is perhaps the most critical. Often a performance problem occurs because a person doesn't know that performance is below standard. Providing feedback about the performance may be all that is needed to return performance to standard. Feedback is a powerful tool for effecting a "positive deviation" with an employee. Research has shown repeatedly that people can become motivated by positive feedback and recognition. And, here again, keeping feedback objective and "process-oriented," ensures its validity and makes it more acceptablle to the recipient.

In spite of these factors, managers can and do develop the skills for dealing effectively with people problems. Some guidelines, as well as some basic principles for managing people appear later in this section. Before reviewing those tips, let's look at Cause Analysis step by step as it applies to the examination of People Problems.

APPLICATION OF THE CAUSE ANALYSIS PROCESS

Step One.   State Problem

Getting off to a good start is particularly important. An accurate, concise statement of the performance deviation gives a solid base for further defining our area of concern. By writing down the expectation and the actual performance, you test this statement for accuracy and appropriateness. The need to separate may become apparent. Also, you become more certain whether a deviation actually exists or is just interpretation.

Ask the following questions to check the problem statement:

1. Is your expectation specific and measurable? (How will you know if it is achieved? What indicators of successful performance can be used?)
2. Is the expectation realistic? (Has anyone ever met it? Does this person have the necessary skills and resources to meet it?)
3. Do all the people involved have the same understanding of the standard?
4. Do the people involved know what their performance is? Are they aware that there is a deviation?

Step Two.   Describe Problem

Use observable behavior (Observed Facts) when describing the problem. Avoid emotional words or generalizations. They confuse the issue since they are opinions rather than the best available facts. For example, the statement "an employee has a bad attitude" may represent your feeling, but is difficult to analyze. By describing the employee's behavior as "the employee is sometimes late to work, hands in some projects late and ignores my instructions," you have more specific statements for your analysis.

It is important to modify process questions when applying them to performance problems. Figure 5.1 presents some applicable process questions. This helps cope with the nature of the information gathering that will be required. Of particular importance is the need to gather the comparative facts to specifically identify those groups/individuals that can be used for comparison.

Step Three.   Identify Differences

Many differences exist among individuals and groups. Physical and psychological distinctions are a fact of life. Since managers have more control over and concern about the work environment; this is the area in which they should look for differences. Specifically, conclusions about people's attitude and motivation are sometimes useless because they are conclusions—NOT FACTS.

Step Four.   List Changes

A characteristic of people is that they can, and often do, absorb change. That is, behavior may not be immediately affected after an environmental modification. People do not always react immediately. We have the capacity to comply with an unpleasant directive and mutter under our breaths and await the next opportunity for revenge. This period of "festering" causes the time involved in Cause Analysis to be severely stretched. The "straw that broke the camel's back" syndrome can develop; we can focus too much on measuring the exact weight of the last straw and ignore the 700 pounds on the now broken back of the camel. It is critical, in searching for changes related to a People Problem, that this be kept in mind and the search for change be expanded in time. Careful attention must be paid to testing causes because of this characteristic.

Step Five.   Generate Likely Causes

A common response to People Problems involves the assessment of blame. Often in attempting to "solve" People Problems, we focus on feelings, attitudes, or personality as a means of finding cause (fault). Look for

PEOPLE PROBLEM ANALYSIS WORKSHEET

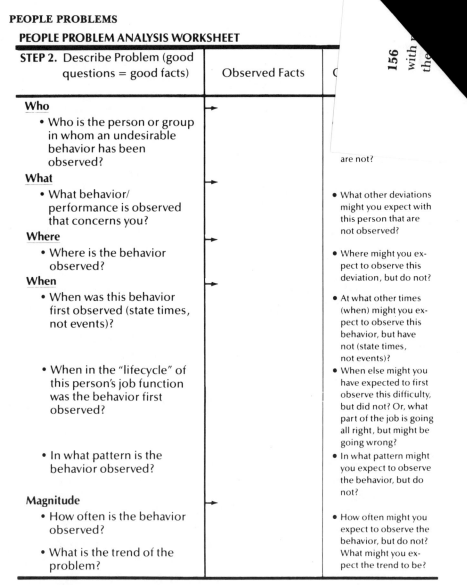

STEP 2. Describe Problem (good questions = good facts)	Observed Facts	
Who • Who is the person or group in whom an undesirable behavior has been observed?		are not?
What • What behavior/ performance is observed that concerns you?		• What other deviations might you expect with this person that are not observed?
Where • Where is the behavior observed?		• Where might you expect to observe this deviation, but do not?
When • When was this behavior first observed (state times, not events)?		• At what other times (when) might you expect to observe this behavior, but have not (state times, not events)?
• When in the "lifecycle" of this person's job function was the behavior first observed?		• When else might you have expected to first observe this difficulty, but did not? Or, what part of the job is going all right, but might be going wrong?
• In what pattern is the behavior observed?		• In what pattern might you expect to observe the behavior, but do not?
Magnitude • How often is the behavior observed?		• How often might you expect to observe the behavior, but do not? What might you expect the trend to be?
• What is the trend of the problem?		

Figure 5.1 Process questions for use in dealing with People Problems.

changes in the environment as keys to cause and always look at people's performance and behavior.

Step Six. Test Likely Causes

In hardware problems, systems and products don't have feelings. If managers try a multitude of solutions to an object ("shotgun problem solving"), they only risk time and money. If they use the same approach people, they risk losing people as well. Therefore, hard testing against problem definition is essential.

Step Seven.   Verify Most Likely Cause

Prior to verifying the most likely cause, take the necessary time to think through:

WHO—should be questioned?

WHAT—information needs to be gathered or verified?

WHERE—should the discussions be held?

WHEN—is the most appropriate time?

MAGNITUDE—How much should be said? How many questions?

Think about the risks associated with the verifying questions and discussions, and prepare accordingly.

Even after we have verified that a cause is accurate and true, we may be limited in our ability to simply apply corrective action. People have memories and feelings. Just because we rationally analyze a series of facts and draw a conclusion about cause does not mean that the feelings that existed during the performance problem will disappear.

How does the new systems analyst feel when the project leader says, "You will be pleased to know that it's not your fault that the debugging is incomplete. I know after all the hassle given to you, that it'll be a relief to put that behind you!"

After three weeks of monitoring, accusation, threats, and other misplaced management activity, the systems analyst cannot simply forget. It's not like changing the battery in a car. The other parts of the car have no memory or feelings about the previous battery. Thus, in managing People Problems, we must fully recognize the implications of the problem solving activity and not assume that cause will lead to simple correction.

Cause Analysis can be used not only to help correct poor performance, but also to give insights into ways to encourage high performance. It is important to look for the "positive deviations"—those times when a person's performance goes above the performance standard. By learning to identify those situations and encourage their repetition, managers can impact the performance and productivity of their organizations and increase their effectiveness as managers.

A Worksheet (Figure 5.2) is provided to assist in analyzing People Problems.

KEY PRINCIPLES OF MANAGING PEOPLE

We have said that process management techniques alone are not the complete answer when dealing with People Problems. The five basic principles discussed in the remainder of this chapter, when practiced in combination with good process skills, will do much to increase a manager's competence to manage people proactively.

Maintain the Self-Esteem of Subordinates

As people feel more confident, performance is improved. Capable managers learn to recognize the opportunity to raise an employee's level of performance by trying to maintain his or her self-esteem. Even when it is necessary to communicate a "negative deviation" in performance to a employee, this principle can be applied. In a discussion of this type, good managers first commend a positive characteristic and then discuss the area that needs improvement, always expressing confidence in the employee's ability to improve.

People tend to fulfill the expectations others hold for them. By expecting and showing that they expect the best from employees, managers have a much better chance of getting it. Destroying the self-esteem of others will guarantee poor performance.

Focus on the Problem Not the Personality

Perhaps because problems involving people are uncomfortable situations, managers often have difficulty focusing on the specific problem in discussions with employees. In a situation where an employee repeatedly arrives late for work, a manager might be tempted to say "You seem to have lost interest in your work. Why can't you be more responsible?" But managers will be more effective and more likely to successfully correct this behavior if they focus their comments on the specific problem, not on the attitude or personality of the employee. Be specific. Describe the magnitude of the problem, for example, "You've been late to work four times in the past two weeks."

By focusing attention on the problem, you allow the employee to remain nondefensive. You can work together on a solution. A discussion about attitude and personality is often vague, often threatening, and the employee may feel that these are things that he or she cannot or will not change. Talk only about the problem or performance, not about the personality.

Use Reinforcement: A Tool to Motivate

The technique of reinforcement to encourage desirable behavior and to discourage undesirable behavior is used with great skill by able managers in business, education, and government. Developing this technique and the ability to recognize opportunities for reinforceement are two valuable aspects in the proactive management of people. Reinforcement, or the conditioning of another person to expect a positive response to desirable actions and a negative response (or no response) to undesirable actions, can be a powerful motivator in shaping people's behavior.

PEOPLE PROBLEM ANALYSIS WORKSHEET

STEP 1. State Problem (include specifically who and what are wrong)

STEP 2. Describe Problem (good questions=good facts)	Observed Facts	Comparative Facts
Who • Who is the person or group in whom an undesirable behavior has been observed? **What** • What behavior/ performance is observed that concerns you? **Where** • Where is the behavior observed? **When** • When was this behavior first observed (state times, not events)? • When in the "lifecycle" of this person's job function was the behavior first observed? • In what pattern is the behavior observed? **Magnitude** • How often is the behavior observed? • What is the trend of the problem?		

OPTIONAL STEP. Examine and Test Experiential Causes

Figure 5.2 Worksheet outlining the

STEP 3. Identify Differences	STEP 4. List Changes	STEP 5. and 6. Generate Likely Causes and Test

STEP 7. Verify Most Likely Cause

steps used in handling People Problems.

A simple example is the salesperson who consistently increases sales and is rewarded in the form of a financial bonus for exceeding previous performance. The salesperson works even harder to continue to elicit a positive response from management—money.

The practice of responding negatively to undesirable behavior is unfortunately the most common form of reinforcement. Take the employee who comes in late to work explaining that because of car trouble it was necessary to arrange another ride to work. Here a skilled supervisor or manager recognizes an opportunity to use the technique of reinforcement in a positive way by acknowledging the extra effort put forth to overcome an obstacle to getting to work. A less skilled manager might see and respond only to the employee's tardiness.

Some guidelines for using reinforcement successfully include:

1. Use extra reinforcement as needed initially because it is more difficult to start behavior change than to sustain it.

2. Avoid waiting for behavior, desirable or undesirable, to become pronounced before responding. Learn to be proactive and to recognize the first signs and reinforce appropriately.

3. Respond (reinforce) immediately following your observation of the behavior. Immediate response has more impact and delayed response can be confusing.

4. Be certain that your reinforcing responses are clear and direct so that they are seen as either positive or negative by the recipient. No one reward or punishment is suitable for everyone. Be careful to select a meaningful reinforcing response.

5. Reduce gradually the frequency of reinforcement after the desired performance level is achieved.

Listen Actively

Active listening refers to the technique of feeding back to a person the information given and the feeling expressed. It is an important skill that can be acquired with practice, and it is especially valuable in emotional exchanges. For example, a salesperson storms into the operations manager's office angrily, stating,

> Your people are incompetent and always slipping schedules! I'm about to lose a key account because you can't do your job of producing this product. What's wrong with you?

An active listener would attempt to respond conveying both the content and the feelings the other person has expressed. Active listening lets the other party know that the listener understands. In this case, the operations manager might have responded nondefensively by nodding and stating calmly,

> You're concerned about a key account and whether or not we can meet the order deadline. It is is important to you and you don't feel Production shares your concern. Let's talk about it and see what we can work out.

Satisfied that she is being heard, the salesperson is open to a discussion to resolve the problem.

Establish Clear Expectations and Keep Communicating

We know that sometimes when an employee is not meeting a performance expectation or goal, it is because the specific expectation has not been clearly communicated. When concluding a meeting with an employee, be certain that the goals have been defined and are understood. And always set a specific date for review, continuing to encourage progress with the employee.

People tend to live up to their self-perceptions. The manager's contribution can be to help raise those levels of self-perception by setting realistic goals and building the employee's self-confidence with continued communication.

CHAPTER 6

Attending Meetings and Assessing Recommendations

So far we have discussed the structuring of a process that is applicable to specific concerns facing the manager. On a day-to-day basis, however, a manager is continually interacting with other people and handling daily concerns not sufficiently important to warrant separate step-by-step process analysis.

If we were to review the daily activities of a manager, we would see that much of a manager's time is not allocated specifically to individual concerns. Instead we would find that much effort and time are absorbed in routine daily activities, for example, reviewing the in-basket, talking with subordinates and peers, meeting with clients or vendors, attending staff meetings, writing reports, and selling ideas to others. The principles of proactive management are applicable to these everyday tasks as well as to specific, analyzable concerns. Since so much time is spent in these ongoing activities, a minimal improvement would yield great dividends.

These daily tasks may be handled in a less-than-optimal manner because they may not be recognized as true management activities. These activities creep into a day though not consciously planned. Therefore, the manager often is in a state of reaction rather than proaction.

In this section, we highlight several typical ongoing activities and suggest how process skills could be applied. The ideas presented are meant to stimulate further thought about how a conscious review of daily activities could result in performance improvement.

SAMPLE MANAGEMENT ACTIVITY LIST

1. Attending meetings.
2. Conducting meetings.
3. Coaching subordinates.
4. Delegating assignments.
5. Counseling others.
6. Writing reports.
7. Reading reports.
8. Keeping up-to-date technologically.
9. Selling ideas/proposals.
10. Reviewing proposals.
11. Developing/monitoring budget.
12. Reviewing/appraising performance.
13. Planning time.
14. Dealing with employees outside their own areas of responsibility.
15. Handling telephone inquiries.
16. Reviewing in-basket items.
17. Completing organization forms.
18. Representing boss/company at meetings and conferences.
19. Planning and reviewing plans.
20. Pursuing professional self-development.

This list is obviously not all-inclusive, but it does represent many of the activities that absorb managerial time. In this chapter we focus on several of these activities to illustrate the application of our ideas. The specific areas we address include: (1) attending meetings, (2) conducting meetings, and (3) assessing recommendations.

We hope that, by the examples shown, the reader will see the applicability of the process skills approach to many of the other items on the management activity list.

ATTENDING MEETINGS

We all attend meetings directed by others. Sometimes they are formal and involve many people; other times they involve only you and one other person. Obviously you have less influence over the meetings you attend than the ones you conduct.

Most managers would say that too much of their time is spent attending meetings. The following case study recounts how one manager tried to improve in this area.

The Case of the Indispensable Attendee

A large manufacturing organization in the Midwest operated under a highly developed set of budgetary controls. As a result, the plant financial controller was in constant demand. No one dared have a meeting without inviting the controller. They never knew whether or not they would require his direction or approval for their plans. As a result, the controller was constantly invited to meetings. In fact, sixty percent of his time was spent attending other people's meetings. This obviously violated his own standard/norm and required action on his part. After seeking and reviewing the causes of his feeling that the meetings were wasting his time, he concluded the following: (1) The meetings had no clear purpose. (2) His role was not clear. (3) He frequently had to leave and get data he didn't realize was going to be required.

Based on these causes, he decided to implement a plan to reduce their effects. He met with his secretary and provided a set of three standard questions to be asked if a request for his attendance at a meeting were received: "Mr. X will be pleased to attend your meeting. However, he would like to know the following:

1. What are the end-results, objectives/purposes of the meeting?
2. What contribution would you like Mr. X to make?
3. What preparation should Mr. X undertake to ensure that the right information is present?"

Based on these questions, several interesting results were realized:

1. In several instances, the person holding the meeting couldn't answer the questions and, therefore, Mr. X didn't attend.
2. In several instances, meetings were canceled.
3. In many instances, Mr. X would attend; however, the results of his attendance improved and he could leave when his part was over.

In three months, the percentages of time spent in the meetings of others dropped to twenty percent.

The message of "The Indispensable Attendee" is quite clear. When managers lack control of a meeting because they are not conducting it, it is critical to protect valuable time and energy. The fact that the managers are not responsible for the success of the meeting does not relieve them of the responsibility of guaranteeing their own effectiveness as participants. The three questions provided are extremely powerful tools to consider even though they will not assure a brave new world of effective meetings. Think of the potential benefits if everyone asked those questions before participating in their next meeting.

CONDUCTING MEETINGS

When we are responsible for conducting meetings, we should be very concerned about achieving results. If managers assessed the dollar cost to organizations of conducting these meetings, they would be astounded. In one research laboratory, where an hourly loaded labor rate is applied for cost control purposes, a calculation of meeting costs was done, as shown in Figure 6.1.

This is a sample situation. If those meetings had been restricted to one hour instead of two, $4200 could have been saved.

Beyond the dollar savings, the results must also be assessed. What was achieved? A survey of participants in the example indicated the meeting was a weekly chore. Most of the data could have been conveyed via a weekly status report and periodic coffee discussions.

Several principles of proactive skills could be applied to improve the effectiveness of the meetings we conduct.

Principle One.   Clarify Purpose

A meeting without a purpose will drift in much the same manner as the process of Decision Making without a clear Decision Statement. A purpose is a statement of the end result objective of the meeting. It always describes the result—not the process for achieving it. For example,

> Purpose 1   To discuss the status of product
>   modification planning.

No matter what happens at that meeting, this purpose can be achieved. There is no obvious end. It could go on forever! In contrast:

Weekly Staff Meeting: Department X

Time:	2 hrs.
Number of people:	6
Hourly loaded rate average:	$35/hr.
One meeting a week:	$210
One year: (estimate: 40 meetings)	$8400

Figure 6.1   An example of how much an ineffective meeting can cost a company on an annual basis.

Purpose 2   To identify any missed milestones on
                   the product modification plan and
                   assign responsibility for actions
                   caused by observed or anticipated
                   deviations.

Notice that, in this instance, the meeting is clearly over when we have
identified what needs to be done and who will do it. As indicated in the case
of "The Indispensable Attendee," this more specific meeting purpose must
also be communicated to all attendees.

Principle Two.   Outline Agenda

Any meeting must have a plan, which, for some reason, is known as an
agenda. The word "plan" is really a better description of what is required.
Whereas an agenda tends to be simple headings and estimated times, a plan
is more definitive. A plan includes the concept of target times, sequential
dependence, and specific responsibility.

In Decision Making, we recognized the need for applying values to our
criteria so that we could make the appropriate trade-offs. The same
principle should apply to meeting plans. Time is the key value applied. The
allocation of time in a meeting should reflect the importance of each
specific agenda item. We have all heard of meetings where one hour is
spent on the color of the paper towels and twenty minutes on the
$1,000,000 planned head office relocation. Thus, in developing meeting
plans, it is critical to first assess the relative value of each item. Some will be
limits; these must be discussed. Others will be only desirables and should be
allocated time according to their importance.

The agenda or meeting plan, in conjunction with the purpose, should
permit individuals to be adequately prepared and the leader to control the
flow of the meeting.

Principle Three.   Maintain Control

The means of controlling a meeting are exactly the same as those used to
control information in the specific proactive management approaches. The
flow of information should follow the logical steps of each individual
process and depend upon the purpose of the meeting. For example:

Situation Review (to analyze what needs to be done)

1. List concerns.
2. Separate concerns.

   3. Establish priorities.

   4. Identify action plans.

Cause Analysis (to find the cause of a problem)

   1. State problem.

   2. Describe problem.

   3. Identify differences.

   4. Examine and test experimental causes (optional).

   5. List changes.

   6. Generate likely causes.

   7. Test most likely cause.

   8. Verify most likely cause.

Decision Making (to select a course of action)

   1. State decision purpose.

   2. Establish decision criteria.

   3. Separate criteria (limits/desirables).

   4. Generate alternatives.

   5. Compare alternatives.

   6. Identify risks.

   7. Assess risks (probability/seriousness).

   8. Make decision.

Plan Analysis (to implement a plan)

   1. State plan briefly.

   2. Select critical steps in plan.

   3. Identify potential problems/opportunities.

   4. Determine likely causes of key potential problems/opportunities.

   5. Determine preventive or facilitative action.

   6. Plan contingent action(s).

   7. Build in alarm(s).

These steps provide a common framework for discussion and permit a meeting to develop efficiently towards its objectives. This is especially true when all persons present are thoroughly familiar with the process steps.

It is important to remember that meetings are not good or bad—they are effective or ineffective. "Meeting" is becoming a dirty word in management circles. This is unfortunate because there are many valid reasons for a group to gather. The inability of managers to effectively achieve outcomes should not result in the condemnation of meetings, but rather of the practices used by meeting leaders.

Proactive skills probably reach their ultimate level of impact as vehicles of achievement at meetings. To validate that statement, managers could tape record a normal meeting and then chart the progress of discussion according to the steps in process. In all probability, managers will discover a blinding, random pattern of inconsistent information processing rather than an orderly, analytical progression along a prescribed process path. The discussion will jump from action to cause to risks to fact gathering to new problems and all around again. Meeting participants will generate their own individual processes in the absence of a group process.

Proactive skills help managers in meetings because they provide a structure for planning and controlling the required data generation and analysis.

ASSESSING RECOMMENDATIONS

Every manager gets involved in evaluating ideas and proposals. The involvement might be as informal as responding to, "What do you think of this idea?" Or it may be as formalized as approving a final proposal submitted by a subordinate or an outside supplier. In assessing proposals, there are two basic concerns: content and logical process.

1. *Content.* The data base on which the proposal is dependent. In the simplest sense, do the numbers add up and is all the right data there? The manager reviewing a proposal is normally competent in the data base involved or has the ability to call in experts for verification.

2. *Process.* The logic or thought processes that were involved in reaching the conclusion. The same data can be organized and structured in many different ways: 2 + 2 can equal 4 or 2 + 2 can equal 22, depending on the process used to manipulate the numbers.

Managers must review both of these factors. We will not attempt to discuss technical expertise; that is the manager's concern. The principles of process management do, however, allow us to discuss the process, or logical flow.

Managers want to know if a proposal has been subjected to some logical analysis or whether it is the result of a subjunctive hunch supported only by carefully chosen facts which are favorable to the proposal.

The following guidelines provide some direction for assessing proposals using proactive skills.

One.   Classify the Proposal

Managers should determine whether they are reviewing a proposed cause, action, or implementation. In most instances, recommendations are proposed actions. If the action is a response to a problem, however, there is a need to review the details of the problem analysis. Managers cannot react to whether adding manpower is better than adding equipment if they don't know what caused the shortage of units in the first place.

Two.   Develop Standard Questions

A major difficulty for a manager assessing proposals is getting the data in simplified form. If subordinates do not know which questions are going to be asked, they will have difficulty organizing the data for review. Fortunately, if managers have classified the proposal, as suggested in Guideline One, they have an easy task developing consistent questions that permit an assessment of the logical flow. The following questions can be used for reviewing each of the three forms of analysis.

CAUSE ANALYSIS

If the proposal to which managers are reacting requires them to assess the accuracy of the Cause Analysis, the following questions can be used:

1. What specific effect are you trying to remove?
2. How did you define the parameters of the effect?
3. What causes did you consider?
4. Why did the other causes fail to explain the effect?
5. How have you checked out the cause you are proposing?

If a subordinate can answer these questions, managers can be assured that considerable thought has been given to the problem.

DECISION MAKING

If managers are required to assess the adequacy of a proposed action, the following questions can be applied:

1. Why is this decision necessary?
2. What key criteria were used in making the choice?

3.   What other alternatives were considered and why is this best?

4.   What risks will we be accepting if we go ahead?

PLAN ANALYSIS

If managers are assessing the quality of thought involved in the implementation of a plan, these are the key questions:

1.   What exactly is the end result of this plan going to be?

2.   What activities are necessary to achieve this?

3.   What could go wrong?

4.   What action will you take to minimize the occurrence of particular problems?

5.   What will you do if the problem occurs and how will you recognize it?

6.   Where might you expect to exceed your goals?

7.   How can you increase the probability of surpassing targets?

The key to assessing proposals is to cause the logic of the proposer to be visible for examination. Binary questions (yes/no) fail to yield any insight into the thought process. The process questions always put the responsibility for analysis on the proposer—where it belongs.

We have attempted to explore the need to consciously build the ideas of proactive management into our daily managing activities. These examples are meant to trigger new thoughts for developing management effectiveness; they are not, however, the only activities that can be improved by proactive management.

Proactive management is common sense. Thinking about what is being done and following a format increases one's ability to utilize management talents to their fullest extent.

CHAPTER 7

Persuasion and Presentation Skills

One of the management implications of the use of process is the ability to use the skills in persuasive situations.

In presenting how an individual can effectively use proactive process in persuasive situations, we reveal two different perspectives. The first is from the point of view of the professional salesperson. The second perspective is that of a manager trying to sell an idea to one or several people of importance in his/her organization.

THE CONSULTATIVE SALES APPROACH

In recent years, most professional sales organizations have attempted to educate their sales people in the Consultative Approach to selling. To most organizations that sell a service, product, or system, the Consultative Approach means that sales people try to understand the needs and problems of their clients and develop a selling strategy before presenting their company's services. They then incorporate a systematic approach to satisfying the client's personal and organizational needs.

In this approach sales people try to establish themselves as problem solvers and/or consultants. Some of the most important skills that Consultative sales people can possess in this endeavor are the abilities to use the Cause Analysis, Decision Making, and Plan Analysis models.

Frequently, organizations have trained their sales people in Cause Analysis so that clients may see them as problem solvers. It is obvious that if a salesperson has the ability to use Cause Analysis in helping clients solve problems, he or she will be strengthening the client relationship. An even

171

stronger relationship develops when both the client and the salesperson have the ability to use Cause Analysis in tackling problems that they have a mutual interest in solving. This bond is greatly strengthened when they are using the same problem solving vocabulary.

One of the largest engineering construction firms in the world provided training in Cause Analysis to most of their consulting engineers who were working on a construction project for a major international oil conglomerate. They knew the oil conglomerate had trained their people in a similar problem solving process and wanted to maintain the effectiveness of their engineers in solving problems that arose while they were building a large regional oil refinery.

As a result of their using the same vocabulary in solving problems on the project, the engineering firm was able to establish a stronger, ongoing relationship with its client. Cause Analysis was not the only process they used in common. They also used the Decision Making Process when they made decisions, and the Plan Analysis Process in constructing the refinery. Preventive and Contingent Action Planning were greatly responsible for the success of the refinery being constructed on schedule and for the development of the maintenance and safety systems for the refinery on a continuing basis.

The effectiveness of any salesperson, selling anything from corporate jets to airline tickets, could be enhanced greatly through the use of the Decision Making Process. The basic fundamental belief in the Consultative Approach to selling is that a salesperson determines and understands the needs of his or her clients. In order to determine the needs of their clients, Consultative Salespeople must ask perceptive questions that will establish the client's confidence. They must communicate a genuine attitude that they want to know the organizational and personal needs of the client and that they understand the client's business and industry.

The Decision Making Process steps are presented to show what Consultative Salespeople should do to maximize the probability of gaining a commitment.

Step One. Determine Where the Client Is in the Decision Making Process and Establish a Decision Statement

This step is extremely important for the following reasons:

1. The prospective client may have already made the decision of whether to buy the salesperson's service or product. If this is the case, the salesperson can save time by getting a contract signed early or by trying to uncover the competitor's weaknesses if the prospective client has tentatively decided on a competitive service.

2. The prospective client may just be shopping around and not really interested in making a commitment.

3.   The prospective client may be at the wrong level in the organization to make a decision and the salesperson's time might be used more effectively elsewhere.

For example, let's suppose a stockbroker was attempting to sell an investment program to a qualified individual. In order for the stockbroker to have proceeded with the sale it would have been important for the stockbroker to have found out what decisions the prospective buyer had already made. If he or she had already narrowed the decision down to high growth appreciation common stocks, it would not have been beneficial for the broker to try to sell the prospective buyer tax free municipals.

In order to find out where the prospective client is in the Decision Making Process, it is necessary to ask the following key questions: Who, What, Where, When, Magnitude. To illustrate how this could be accomplished, the following questions might have been asked by the stockbroker:

1.   *WHO?*   Are the decisions for investments in your organization or family made by one person or a committee? Who is/are this person(s)?
2.   *WHAT?*   What kind of investments have you felt you would be interested in? What kinds of investments have you made a satisfactory return in recently?
3.   *WHEN?*   When do you wish to invest?
4.   *WHERE?*   Where do you expect to do business?
5.   *MAGNITUDE?*   What amount of funds do you have to invest? How often would you expect to make this kind of an investment?

Let's say the answers to the above questions were the following:

1.   *WHO?*   Yes, it is my responsibility to make the final investment decision for my company/family.
2.   *WHAT?*   Common stocks of small high technology companies.
3.   *WHEN?*   Immediately.
4.   *WHERE?*   Southern California. Presently, we do business in California, but hope to expand to several other locations in North America.
5.   *MAGNITUDE?* $80,000. Probably every other year.

At this point the broker probably would have felt he or she had a well-qualified prospective client at the right level of the Decision Making Process. The broker might have determined with confidence that the prospective client's Decision Statement would be: To invest $80,000 in common stocks with a rapid-growth potential immediately.

Step Two.   Establish the Needs of the Client; Why Are They Buying?

Once the Decision Statement had been established (and the prospective client further qualified), it was time for the stockbroker to begin exploring the prospective client's Decision Criteria or needs. Suppose in our example that the broker helped clarify the needs of the prospective client based on questions like, "What rate of return do you require?" "How much discretionary money do you plan to invest in the foreseeable future?" and, "What kind of risk are you willing to take in different economic climates?"

Many times in the brokerage industry and others, prospective clients may not be readily able to articulate all of their needs. This works to the salesperson's advantage by providing other opportunities to be consultative; in our example, by helping the prospective client make the criteria that will influence the ultimate decision visible.

Suppose in our example that the stockbroker was able to extract the following needs and criteria from the prospective client:

1. Willing to speculate.
2. Would prefer capital gains.
3. Has no immediate income requirements from the funds.
4. Is interested in rapid growth companies.
5. Would like to invest in the electronics industry.
6. Would like companies in the western part of North America.

Step Three.   Present the Alternative that Best Satisfies the Limits and Desirable Needs of the Client

After having determined the client's needs and followed the Decision Making Process, the stockbroker determined an alternative that would meet the needs of the client. The portfolio recommendation has to meet needs that are Limits and satisfy as well as possible those that are Desirables.

Obviously this entire process was being worked through during a give-and-take presentation by the stockbroker and the prospective client. If the broker had gained the confidence of the prospect the final proposal would have been arrived at by mutual agreement. If the broker's proposal didn't satisfy the needs of the prospective client, competition would likely have entered the picture. If he or she hadn't solicited another broker to present alternative investment portfolios, the prospective client would have been scoring either unconsciously or consciously the alternatives against his or her Decision Making Criteria.

Step Four.   Present a Risk Analysis Describing a Plan for Dealing with Things that Could Go Wrong

If the client is concerned about things that might go wrong, it is valuable for the salesperson to go into the Plan Analysis Process. It is important for the salesperson to point out how potential problems can be prevented. But if they do arise, well-thought-out Contingent Actions can be implemented to minimize the possibility of their becoming major problems that could destroy the success of the selection; for example, as in the case of the stockbroker, sell options could be purchased for certain volatile stocks in the portfolio.

The salesperson who presents the alternative that best satisfies the client's needs and has the smallest risk will usually win the prospective client's business. Again the prospective client may not go through the formal Decision Making Process, but he or she will go through some of their own processes, at least mentally. If the Consultative Salesperson is confident he or she has the best alternative over the competition, it is advantageous to make the Decision Making Process as formal as possible. A flow chart for Consultative Selling is presented in Figure 7.1.

PRESENTATION SKILLS

Whether people are in business, medicine, law, or any other profession, probably one of the most important things they do is communicate. In the communicating process, people (and especially managers) sell their ideas. New ideas are the source of growth and excitement. They can produce startling results for an organization. Any successful company competing in today's business environment must be receptive to new ideas.

Unfortunately, many new ideas are never pursued because people are not able (or are afraid) to convince others in the organization of the utility of those new thoughts. And, conversely, threatened by change, many managers do not reward innovative thinking by their subordinates. Therefore, the following discussion of presentation skills with the use of process could help avoid these pitfalls.

Preparation

If a manager has a good working understanding of process skills and the ability to sell his or her ideas, the probability of being a successful manager is increased immeasurably. The ability to persuade others is probably the single most common trait among successful business people. Some key things to remember in preparing for a presentation are the following:

1. Managers should know where the person or group is in the Decision Making Process before making a presentation. A manager should

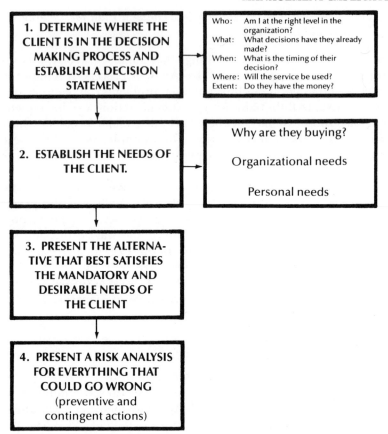

Figure 7.1 Flowchart outlining the Consultative Sales Approach.

know the answer to the question, "What decisions have been made in the past with respect to the alternative I'm presenting?" For example, a manager doesn't want to be selling his or her boss the idea that top executives should fly first class when the boss is already considering the purchase of a new corporate jet for executive travel.

2. It is important to know the needs of the person or group to whom a manager is selling an idea. As in the Consultative Approach to selling, managers will be more successful selling an idea if they know the needs or the Decision Making Criteria of the person or group to whom they are selling. Additionally, the more information managers have about questions that may come up, the more comfortable they will feel when delivering their presentations.

3. Managers should be prepared to minimize the risks of their alternatives or solutions. It is helpful to go through the Plan Analysis Process and be prepared to present Preventive Actions that will

eliminate problems. Contingent Actions should also be ready for presentation if something should go wrong with the plan.

4. Change is threatening. Thus if managers are presenting new ideas, they must minimize the perceived threat to those hearing the presentation.

5. An idea that makes the manager a winner and someone else a loser probably isn't a very good idea. In the long run it may do the manager more damage than good. It would be worthwhile to ask some "How will . . .?" questions before putting a new idea into action. "How will the implications of this idea affect my manager? My peers? My subordinates?" and, of course, "How will it affect the organization?"

The Presentation

Once the homework is finished and the presentation is ready, there are nine basic points to keep in mind in order to make an effective presentation.

1. Review the intent of the presentation. There are several basic reasons for making a presentation: (1) to motivate, (2) to persuade, (3) to inspire, (4) to entertain, and (5) to inform.
   The first three types of presentation require action on the part of the audience. The presenter is trying to get them to do something. A format for this kind of presentation is shown in Figure 7.2.
   The last two types of presentation require no action on the part of the audience. In these formats the presenter is describing one or several items or topics. A chart for these presentations is on Figure 7.3.

2. Try to be yourself. Most people fail as presenters when they try to be something they are not. Their presentations come across as artificial and turn out to be a failure.

3. Have confidence in yourself. This is probably the most important part of any presentation. If presenters are not self-assured and confident, the audience will sense it and lose the message of what is being presented.

4. Use extended eye contact. Look directly into the eyes of as many people as you can for about four to five seconds during your presentation.

5. Let gestures be natural. Be loose. Be relaxed. Some people pretend they are at a cocktail party talking to *one* of their close friends. Appropriate gestures come automatically when people are excited about what they are presenting.

Format for Persuasion, Motivation, and Inspiration Presentations

---

Goals of Presentation

- What is it you want to achieve?

Motivation

- What is in it for the audience?

Need

- Perceived decision making criteria of audience.

Solutions

- Alternatives or a range form impractical to most desirable.

Risks

- Describe preventive and contingent actions.

Action Step

- Who and how to take the first step?

Figure 7.2 Outline format for persuasion presentations.

6. Tell stories and give examples to make a point. The more good examples used in a presentation, the more effective and interesting the communication. Understanding will be clearer if the audience has a concrete example to which they can relate.

7. Dress appropriately for the occasion. A person's visual appearance is extremely important. If people don't know a presenter, they may tune out entirely if the person is not appropriately dressed. If ever in question about attire, always overdress instead of underdress. People are better received if they are dressed formally at an informal gathering than informally at a formal gathering. A weak presentation content can frequently be overcome by making a professional appearance and delivery.

8. Use natural voice in delivery. As in the use of gestures, the key here is to be natural. However, be careful not to talk too slow, too fast, or in a monotone or trail off at the end of a sentence. Again, being confident is essential for successful delivery. The old adage still holds to some extent, "It's not what you say but how you say it."

In conclusion, managers who have a good use of proactive process and the skills for making good presentations have the ability to motivate, persuade, and ultimately be more effective managers. Sales professionals are perceived to be especially valuable to their clients if they acquire the use of

---
Format for Information, Teaching, and Entertaining Presentations
---

Objective:
- What do you hope to achieve?

Motivation:
- What is in it for the audience?

Overview:
- General description of the topic, including a list of component parts.

Specific Points:

Point #1:
- What:
- Why:
- How:
- Example:
- Test understanding:

Point #2:
- What:
- Why:
- How:
- Example:
- Test understanding:

Summary

Figure 7.3 Outline format for information presentation.

process to determine their clients' needs, and then present alternatives that satisfy those needs. Finally, one of the most persuasive skills anyone can possess is the ability to assure others that he or she has a good grasp of what could go wrong and is prepared to minimize the risks involved in taking any particular course of action.

DEVELOPING PROACTIVE SKILLS IN OTHERS

This section is directed to individuals responsible for developing the managerial skills and capabilities of other people. We believe that includes all managers. Unfortunately, many organizations allocate that responsibility solely to a corporate management development department. Of course, this department plays a very important role within a company; however, the ultimate responsibility for training should be the manager's.

The proactive approach to dealing with management responsibilities has special implications for those concerned with developing managerial talent. A challenge arises from the fact that proactive management is an attempt to elevate an unconscious thinking process to a visible information processing system. Normally in the development of managerial skills we are able to focus on fairly objective, visible systems or mechanisms, for example, how to conduct a performance appraisal, how to conduct a selection interview, how to develop a one-year and three-year plan. These are typical of specific managerial activities that must be performed well if a manager is to be successful. Proactive management, however, does not fall into the traditional classification of a managerial activity. Rather, it encompasses all management activity without being restricted to any level, time, or specific task.

Proactive management is a method for formalizing common sense and logic within the managerial environment. Traditionally, the acquisition or development of common sense was assumed to be genetic. That is, you either had it or you did not. While we do not claim that proactive

181

management can replace good instincts, we do strongly believe that these skills can improve judgment. Good problem solving and decision making are a combination of good data, properly classified and assessed alternatives, and an adequate assessment of risks. Proactive skills ensure that these steps are minimally included in any decision. While experience applied at each stage remains valuable, the raised visibility produced by proactive skills can increase objectivity.

Henry Mintzberg, in his book *The Nature of Managerial Work* (1977), raises some very important and insightful questions that all managers should consider. Basically, Mintzberg challenges the traditional definition of managerial work. He questions the validity of planning, controlling, budgeting, directing, and so on as the key functions of an executive. Mintzberg claims that if we followed a manager around day-to-day, minute-by-minute, we would discover that these traditional functions are not prevalent. His comments are based on extensive research in which he attached himself to key executives and watched their behavior and activity over periods of time. Among other conclusions, he determined that a prime requisite for success at the managerial level is the skill of "information processing." He is not talking about computers. He is talking about the ability to generate, classify, analyze, and evaluate data—essential components of proactive skills.

With the current information explosion, the need for a systematic process for analyzing data has increased. As management develops, the need for teaching new managers to cope with increased amounts of data also increases. It is incumbent on any organization to consciously develop these skills in key employees. Unfortunately, reading this book or others like it will not be enough. Skill building does not occur through intellectual awareness alone. It comes from a planned approach to learning and from managing the learning process. The roles and responsibilities of the manager and the management development specialist in this learning process are developed in this section.

CHAPTER 8

The Role of the Manager in Developing Proactive Skills in Others

In the development of skills and the application of skills for performance, there is no single more important element than the individual manager. The role model and expectations of the manager have been determined to be the single most influential factor affecting employee performance. We learn most of our basic skills through observation of role models. We learn to talk, walk, behave in public, and other necessary key skills by constant observation of others around us. Parents provide role models in the development of children. Research on the impact of various parent behaviors indicates the extreme importance of modeling behavior. A brief example is the use of language. Repeated tests have shown that parents who speak to children using proper words and pronunciations tend to improve the capability of young children to build appropriate vocabulary very early. Parents who talk "baby talk" to children tend to inhibit the early development of speech patterns and skills.

CREATING A POSITIVE ROLE MODEL AND HIGH EXPECTATIONS

Managers provide role models for their subordinates. If they shoot from the hip, jump to cause, or push favorite alternatives, they must expect their subordinates to operate in a similar fashion. How managers operate as managers directly affects how subordinates operate as workers and ultimately as managers.

Beyond role modeling, another influential factor affecting performance is managerial expectation. If we expect our subordinates to be on time, they tend to be on time. If we expect detailed analysis, we tend to get detailed analysis. If we expect a rational analysis rather than an educated guess, we tend to get that analysis. Subordinates have an amazing ability to "figure out" the boss. Just as you know your boss's "hot buttons," your subordinates have identified yours.

In a *Harvard Business Review* article entitled "Pygmalion in Management" (1969), Sterling Livingston describes the impact of managerial expectation on employee performance. He argues convincingly that what we expect of employees can directly affect their level of performance. Subordinates are capable of rising to the occasion, of growing and developing. If managers conveniently confine people in rigid, labeled boxes, they correspondingly restrict their growth. Definitions such as "winner, loser, slow, and peaked" are difficult to remove once applied. It is critical to assess the ongoing validity of such labels because people change.

Let us assume that you, the reader, are a successful manager. That is an applied label that creates an expectation of performance in your mind. Yet, were you always so labeled? Were there times when you were labeled something else . . . trainee, up-and-coming, steady, dependable, satisfactory, or even "average"? What you were five to ten years ago is not what you are today. What your subordinates are today is not what they will be in five to ten years. One of them will probably be in *your* job.

The development of people is a critical responsibility for managers. Unfortunately, it is often left to the individual to determine key learning points, internalize the learning, and extend it to performance. "The cream will rise to the top" is the organization's response. Even the smallest dairy farmer knows that while this is true, it is also ridiculously inefficient and time consuming. A farmer facilitates the process by purchasing a separator to ensure that a predictable amount and quality of cream is obtained. Managers must do the same thing. They must facilitate and manage the development of talent, not wait for its ultimate appearance by chance. To do this requires a consciously managed learning process. It also requires an understanding of how people learn and how managers interact with that learning process.

UNDERSTANDING AND USING A LEARNING MODEL

There are many theories about how people learn. For the purpose of considering proactive skills and exploring the role of the manager, we explore a simplified four-stage learning model. The basic model has four stages that represent the individual's stages of competence. First let us develop the full model (as shown on Figure 8.1) and then explore each stage for the role of the manager.

Stage One.   *Unconscious Incompetence*

In this state of being, individuals do not realize that their performance is not as required or desired. The learners do not know they don't know. This stage is a major stumbling block to development. Subordinates who are not aware of their need to improve cannot improve. While physical skills are obvious to people, some of the more difficult skills (like using proactive management, writing letters, and running meeetings) are more subtle. Subordinates might not be aware of the fact that they need improvement in some of these less visible skills. The critical first step in managing the development of subordinates in proactive management is to direct the individual's perception to the second stage: conscious incompetence.

Stage Two.   *Conscious Incompetence*

How does a person move from stage one to stage two? There is only one method: feedback. That feedback can be either self-analysis or external feedback. This latter is the prime role of the manager. It is critical for the manager to accurately monitor and assess the problem solving and decision making skills of subordinates. As deficiencies or problems develop, the manager should discuss and provide feedback to ensure the subordinate is aware of both expectations and current performance level.

Many managers claim they already do this in performance appraisal programs. Such evaluations, however, generally focus on results, not process, and are too far removed from the day-to-day behavior that must be modified.

Feedback is critical to learning, but it does not by itself produce learning. Feedback, if accepted and valid, creates an awareness in the mind of the subordinate, "I need to do better." In other words, conscious incompetence. *Caution:* we are not talking about total incompetence, but rather a specific skill deficiency.

Learning Model

Unconscious Incompetence

↓

Conscious Incompetence

↓

Conscious Competence

↓

Unconscious Competence   **Figure 8.1**   Common stages of learning in skill building.

There are several methods a manager can use to give feedback on proactive skills. One approach is to select specific projects, assignments, or decisions and consciously monitor their progress, providing feedback at key steps of the appropriate proactive management process. This technique creates extra work for the manager and places total responsibility for development on the manager, rather than on the learner. A second approach is to systematically assess the skill level of the subordinate on a predeveloped breakdown of proactive skills. This approach needs some elaboration.

As has been demonstrated, proactive management is not a single skill. It is a composite set of skills. Performance levels vary at different steps of each process. Some subordinates are great at generating alternatives but have trouble assessing risk. Some excel in decision making, but are less able in implementation. To develop each subordinate appropriately means first identifying the strengths and weaknesses at each step of proactive management. The identification of improvement areas would be strengthened if the subordinate participated in that assessment.

The list shown in Figure 8.2 is a breakdown of each step in the four processes described in proactive management.

Upon completion of this skill checklist, the manager and subordinate can meet and compare their assessments. Of particular concern will be three possible results:

1. *Strengths.* The manager and subordinate agree upon the existence of a highly developed skill. This can be a vehicle for providing further growth opportunities for the individual.

2. *Agreed Skill Deficiencies.* The manager and subordinate agree that a particular step or steps of proactive management need improvement. Specific areas should be fully explored and taken to the next stage: conscious competence.

3. *Assessment Disagreements.* The manager and the subordinate disagree about the level of skill. For the purpose of discussion, a differential of two points is considered to be a disagreement. Such differences should be discussed to determine their validity. Two possible situations exist. First, the subordinate could be in a stage of unconscious incompetence and unaware of a need to do better. In this case, the manager must provide specific feedback to develop increased awareness. Second, the subordinate could be correct and the manager wrong. In this instance, the manager should back off and look for areas where there is agreement on the need to improve.

Stage Three.   Conscious Competence

This state of performance represents the fragile existence of recently learned skills. Learners know what they are supposed to do and can perform the task in a controlled manner. At this level, the performance requires conscious effort and thought. It is like new golfers just after a lesson. All the time they are addressing the ball, messages are going through their brains. On the tee, you can watch the golfers go through mental checklists: hands, feet, arms, shoulders, and so on. This is conscious competence: knowing how to do something, but needing time and thought to perform adequately.

This is obviously a higher level than conscious incompetence. The central question becomes, "How do you move a subordinate from conscious incompetence to conscious competence?" The answer is through planned learning input. This could be a course, a book, individual discussions, one-on-one coaching, or a range of other learning mechanisms. At this point, the manager and the training specialist begin to interact. If the skill that needs to be developed is singular and within the competence of the manager, it is most efficient and effective for the manager to simply instruct the subordinate. If, however, it is a complex skill, or a whole range of skills, the training and development specialist might be used to identify alternative means of skill building. The training department might be conducting an ongoing basic program aimed at the specific skills requiring development.

It is important to note that training, in any form, can only progress a learner to a level of conscious competence. This is a delicate state because it requires thought and effort. People frequently forget or get tired of learning and begin to reverse the learning sequence. For learning to achieve its ultimate goal, it must be directed to the fourth stage: unconscious competence.

Stage Four. Unconscious Competence

This state of performance can be described as doing it right without even thinking about it. Good performance at that skill is achieved as a matter of habit. Learners are free to concentrate on their jobs rather than on their skills. This breakthrough is required if performance is to be modified into a new, positive level of achievement. It's an exciting state of performance. It's like the first time you ski a hill and enjoy it because you did it naturally, rather than thoughtfully. It's like the first backhand return in tennis that flow easily rather than as a six-step movement. Doing it properly is now the new expectation. It is no longer a big deal.

The essential question remains, "How do you arrive at this advanced stage?" How do you progress a subordinate to the level of unconscious competence? The answer lies in the role of the manager. The training division can no longer be responsible. Only two things create this critical transition: practice and reinforcement.

A skill that is learned must be reinforced by practice, repetition, and ongoing feedback. After a training input, the manager must *expect* the subordinate to utilize these skills. Training courses very seldom change behavior. They simply provide the basic knowledge or skill that can be

Scoring Directions: Independently, a manager and subordinate should assess the individual's current skill level and the importance of each process step, using a 1-5 scale. Use some 5's and 1's as appropriate; making everything a 3 will not provide adequate feedback.

Skill Importance

5 = Absolutely essential to job success
4 = Important to job success
3 = Part of job requirements
2 = Sometimes important in job
1 = Not relevant or part of job

Skill Level

5 = A highly developed skill, a definite strength
4 = A skill carried out better than most other people
3 = Satisfactory performance of that skill
2 = Needs some improvement
1 = Does not use this skill or does not have this skill

Figure 8.2   Assessment sheet for Proactive Management Skills.

taken back to the jobs. Whether this new knowledge and skill are applied on the job depends on the learned and his or her boss. Trainees frequently get feedback from graduates of formal training programs about the diifficulties of getting support on the job. As subordinates attempt to apply skills learned in training sessions, they are sometimes met with scorn or ridicule. Comments may include, "You will have to forgive Sandra, she has been to a seminar. She will be back to normal soon!" When this occurs, the subordinate will never go beyond conscious competence. In many instances the learner will even have a difficult time staying at that level.

The investment required to train subordinates in any skill is considerable in both time and dollars. If it is worth that investment, surely it must be worth the effect of selecting a few key projects, assignments, or activities and reinforcing the skills that have been developed. Who in their right minds would spend their own money and time on tennis lessons if they never identified when they might someday play tennis? Likewise, no one should develop management skills if he or she cannot apply them.

A central factor influencing performance is managerial expectation, as mentioned earlier. This is a prime example of how the manager's expectation can influence behavior. If the manager begins to expect and demand demonstrated results from proactive skill development, it will occur. Thus, developing the ability of subordiantes in Situation Review, Cause Analysis, Decision Making and Plan Analysis is a fundamental responsibility of every manager. The development of these skills must be a managed process involving specific behavior on the part of the manager to facilitate that development. Managers need not be experts in the content of the learning; however, they must be committed to making the learning process work.

	Skill Importance	Current Skills Level
Situation Review		
• Identify and list concerns		
• Separate/clarify concerns		
• Establish priorities		
• Determine starting point for analysis		
Cause Analysis		
• State problem		
• Describe problem		
• Identify differences		
• List changes		
• Generate likely causes		
• Test most likely cause		
• Verify most likely cause		
Decision Making		
• State decision purpose		
• Establish decision criteria		
• Separate criteria		
• Generate alternatives		
• Compare alternatives		
• Identify risks		
• Assess risks		
• Make decision		
Plan Analysis		
• Select critical areas in plan		
• Identify potential problems/ opportunities		
• Determine likely causes of key potential problems/opportunities		
• Develop preventive/facilitative action(s)		
• Plan contingent action(s)		
• Build in alarm(s)		

Figure 8.2   Continued

The Role of the Management Development Specialist in Developing Proactive Skills in Others

The training and development specialist plays a significant role in developing proactive skills in others within the organization. In this chapter we explore how the uniqueness of proactive skills affects the training specialist.

STRUCTURING PROACTIVE SKILL DEVELOPMENT

We discuss the implications and responsibilities of the specialist in terms of several critical training activities: (1) identifying training needs, (2) selecting the population, (3) grouping the participants, (4) timing the training, and (5) selling the training.

Identifying Training Needs

Identifying appropriate training needs that are relevant to proactive management is more difficult than a similar assessment for a single, easily observable skill. A training specialist can easily determine training needs when describing physical skills, for example, "Can you drive a fork-lift truck?" Where numerical results are available, it is also easy to assess needs, for example, "How many accidents involving fork-lift truck operators are reported in a month?" It is more complicated to ask "What is the need for better problem definition, more complete risk analysis, or more conscious appreciation of potential problems and opportunities?"

A traditional source of training needs in an organization is performance appraisals or reviews. Normally, there is a column or box, hidden on page three in a corner, asking, "What training is required by this employee?" Unless managers have a background in training needs analysis, it would be wise to ignore most data collected in this manner. Often the identified training is based only on known existing training courses and programs. In other words, this information doesn't tell you the need; it describes the solution. The following examples demonstrate the apparent confusion between assessing needs and providing solutions.

Performance Appraisal Example

A major computer company had a very highly regarded performance appraisal and review system. Of particular pride was the discussion on the training needs between boss and subordinate. As part of the audit of this system, a training consultant pulled fifty random performance appraisals from the files of over 1000 people. In each case, a course was listed as the training need. In forty-eight out of fifty instances the courses listed were identified as those currently offered by the training department. Further discussions with the managers involved confirmed that they used a copy of the company training schedule as the basis for discussing needs. The extent of the discussion was usually "Which course have you not yet taken?"

Training Schedule Example

A major company's training division noticed that eighty percent of the requests for the training schedule occurred in the two weeks prior to the annual performance review. Thus, programs were filled because they were advertised. Needs were not discussed; courses were.

Some organizations now have eliminated the request for "What training is required?" and have substituted "What specific skills should be developed?"

Many large corporations use assessment centers as a vehicle for determining the needs of managers. An assessment center is basically a controlled environment where candidates are asked to perform basic management activities in a mythical company. It is a particularly valid tool for assessing proactive skills because individuals are assessed not only for the results of their performance, but also on the process they applied. By constant monitoring and observation, trained assessors can readily make judgments about the degree of development of proactive skills.

While a major use of assessment centers is the identification and development of candidates for "fast track" promotion routes, they provide hope for the future in gathering better data on what skills should also be developed. A training and development specialist trained as an assessor can translate important information about existing or needed skills back into the organization's training program.

Another mechanism for identifying training needs in proactive skills is individual interviews and observation of working managers and groups. The key to proper identification of training needs lies in the workplace. It is not found on organization charts, forms, or spreadsheets. The training specialist must get out into the operation, talk to people, observe how the job gets done. The specialist also must keep track of developments that may influence current training programs. The following example demonstrates the failure to do this.

The training director of a major company established a corporate program to train all regional managers and unit managers in effective Decision Making skills. Seventy-five percent of the way through the program it was discovered that the general manager had recently developed a new comprehensive unit manager standard operating procedure text. The purpose of this document was to remove ninety percent of the discretion from the jobs of the unit manager. All managers would have to do now was "look it up in the book." There would be no need for individual decision making at that level. All the investment and effort in training unit managers in Decision Making was a waste of time and only served to increase the frustration of that group.

Training specialists trained in proactive skills should be able to gather the critical data about the problem solving and decision making abilitites of groups simply by watching them operate. In many instances, the objectivity provided by an outsider can be useful to the manager and the subordinates in identifying needs for development.

Selecting the Population

Population identification is an extension of the training need identification process. A thorough review of the people at each level and within each group should be carried out to develop a composite list of potential training participants. The straight mass listing of names without consideration of individuals could create problems in the training activity. Many times trainers find people listed for training two weeks before retirement, or transfer, or termination. In these instances, names and not people are being trained.

A second feature of selecting the appropriate population is to ensure that all those involved in problem solving and decision making in the company are included in the training. Current emphasis in management theory indicates that problem solving responsibility is best located at the level closest to the problem. Thus we have found that training key operators, lead hands, clerks, tellers, machine operators, among others, in problem solving has paid off handsomely for companies. In identifying the population, a training specialist should consider "information sources" as well as "information analysts." The main point is to identify those who will be involved in solving the problem, not only those with the responsibility to resolve it.

Grouping the Participants

In developing proactive skills programs, a training specialist might use criteria different from other kinds of training programs. In some areas, it is critical to avoid boss-subordinate relationships within the training programs. This protects the ego of the boss and provides a risk-free environment for the subordinate. In developing proactive skills, however, it may be desirable to train full working groups including boss and subordinates. If the skills are going to be applied on the job, the group must get practice in working with the process together. What better place than the training program where it is structured and relatively risk-free?

Because proactive skill training involves the resolution of real concerns and problems, it is preferable to have the key people present during a seminar or course. Thus grouping should be around the existence of ongoing problems for the ultimate group utilization of process.

Timing the Training

In discussing the role of the manager, we emphasized the need for practice and application to create unconscious competence. Timing is also an important variable in learning. Since the level of a skill will deteriorate over time without practice, it is critical to focus all working members of groups into a compressed time period. Any administrative inconvenience is far outweighed by the improved results. The stretching of training over large time periods is not recommended. Research indicates that a three-day format is most effective with follow-up and reinforcement every three to six months until unconscious competence is achieved.

Selling the Training

This leads to the last but probably most critical role in structuring training. The training specialist must sell. The sending out of memos will not be sufficient to gain the involvement of essential managers. The training specialist will have to gather the supporting data and sell managers on the need and method for process training. Most managers are proud of the way they solve problems and make decisions (even if they can't describe how they do it). They will not necessarily support the need for process training just because the training specialist recommends it. The skills and strategies of selling ideas are critical skills for good training specialists.

BECOMING AN INTERNAL CONSULTANT IN PROACTIVE SKILLS

Perhaps no other single follow-up activity in training has the impact of consulting in proactive skill application. It should be the objective of any process training specialist to generate as much consulting as teaching activity within the organization.

Process consulting activity requires a very specialized and difficult set of skills. The consultant must be willing to deal with a high degree of uncertainty while working with managers who are content experts but not necessarily process experts. The uncertainty is derived from the unfamiliarity with the specific information that is the specialty of the manager. The manager is the expert in the subject matter. The consultant's job is to help the manager ask questions, clarify responses, and stay on a proper analytical track. It remains the responsibility of the managers to find their own solutions, make their own decisions, and implement their own plans. Managers must be left with the skills to solve their own problems. There are more problems out there than any consultant could ever solve. Therefore, the process consultant must find satisfaction through the achievement of others.

There are two fundamental elements that the process consultant must consider. First, there is the establishment of a capability and a recognition that would cause managers to ask for process assistance. Second, there is the development of the range of intervention skills necessary to carry out that assignment effectively.

In establishing credibility, there is no more powerful tool than the training program. During a proactive skill training program, a course leader has the opportunity to demonstrate skill level and the ability to provide services. If course participants see benefit in a course leader's assistance and guidance, they will ask for help in real life. The training room provides the opportunity for managers to observe the skills and capabilities of the training specialist. A memo or announcement from a training manager that describes the new training role of consulting has never impressed a line manager yet! What does impress managers is actually getting help and assistance. Properly designed training programs provide this as a minimum objective.

Using Diverse Intervention Methods

The process consultant has a wide range of tools available for use in the consulting situation. Part of the difficulty of being an effective consultant is knowing which tools to use at different times. Process consultants label these tools "interventions." Because the process consultant wants to aid rather than take over the problem, it's critical to consider the optimum intervention technique. Several possible techniques available to the process skills consultant briefly described here include: (1) subjective-based, (2) time-based, (3) process development-based, (4) control-based, (5) feedback-based, and (6) agenda-based.

SUBJECTIVE-BASED INTERVENTION

This type of intervention occurs when the manager/client and consultant agree, based on perceived needs, that the process can be interrupted. There are two variations of this type. Primarily, there is subjective, client-based intervention. In this instance, managers/clients will ask for assistance whenever they feel help is needed. The consultant is totally dependent upon the manager/client's perceiving difficulties and feeling the need for assistance. While minimizing unnecessary interruptions by the consultant, this method can produce difficulties if the manager/client is too committed to a particular direction before asking for help.

The second variation is subjective, consultant-based intervention. In this case, the manager/client gives the process consultant absolute freedom to intervene and provide assistance wherever the consultant perceives the need. This demonstration of faith by the manager must not be abused by the consultant. The process consultant must remember the task focus of the manager/client and not let too lengthy an analysis impede progress.

TIME-BASED INTERVENTION

This is basically a technique where the client and consultant agree on a fixed schedule of intervention. It is the easiest to negotiate because it allows managers/clients to proceed toward their goals with a provision for stopping and checking their process at fixed intervals. The process check that occurs at the scheduled process break should focus on what has happened in the preceeding interval and how to maximize the next time frame.

Time-based intervention is simple and easy to sell; there are times, however, when it's difficult to designate specific time frames as natural breakpoints. There are times, when, say, the manager/client is involved in a weighty issue, that are absolutely inappropriate for a process check. This method can often be used in combination with a third type of intervention.

PROCESS-DEVELOPMENT-BASED INTERVENTION

This type of intervention requires the manager/client and consultant to have a common understanding of the steps in the particular process being used. Basically they agree on a consultant intervention based on progress in the process steps. For example, if the manager/client were in a Decision Making role, she or he might negotiate a planned intervention at the end of each process step: decision purpose, decision criteria, decision alternatives, risk analysis, and final choice.

Rather than time being the basis for intervention, the manager/client can focus on each process step as an individual activity and receive feedback and assistance prior to advancing to the next step. This is one of the most valuable types of intervention because of the focus on manager/client rather than consultant behavior. The role of the process consultant is very much the role of the coach between periods of a hockey game or halftime at a football game.

CONTROL-BASED INTERVENTION

Frequently a manager/client will ask for help or assistance and expect the consultant to take over responsibility for process. Often this is introduced by the phrase "Why don't you take the pen/chalk and run us through that process of yours? We think it might help us!" The manager/client expects the consultant to direct the information analysis.

Although sometimes unavoidable, this intervention is not recommended as the ongoing basis of a manager/consultant relationship. The manager/client is not learning how to process problems and decisions. The consultant is doing it instead, thus creating an undesirable dependency. When this situation is inescapable, it should be converted into an opportunity to convince others of the validity and value of process.

FEEDBACK-BASED INTERVENTION

This type of intervention is characterized by a high degree of nonactivity. The manager/client and consultant agree on the simple observation of a group with no interruptions permitted. When the task is completed, the consultant provides process feedback to either the group as a whole or to the manager/client.

This intervention has marginal value as a process consulting role. By taking notes and observing the group, the consultant already is intervening and affecting group process. Group members often worry more about what the consultant is writing down than about achieving results. Also, feedback is meaningless unless it can be projected into new behavior. Unless the group observed is going to meet again immediately, there is a danger that the feedback will be forgotten by the time they meet again. Telling people does not modify behavior. It only affects their awareness of the need to change performance.

AGENDA-BASED INTERVENTION

This intervention is focused on decreasing the manager/dependency on the consultant. The manager/client and consultant take time before a meeting to plan the agenda and discuss process implications. By spending time up front, the consultant's objective is to ensure that the manager/client knows exactly what to do, how to deal with expected problems, how to manage the process, and how to achieve the desired results. In this instance, the process consultant doesn't even go to the meeting. The manager/client is able to operate independently, based on the agenda and structure planned previously with the consultant.

This is a true process consulting. The manager/client is totally independent and receiving assistance and coaching in the planning mode rather than the doing mode. The manager/client soon becomes independent because of the development at the unconscious competence level.

The role of the management development specialist in developing proactive skills in others encompasses many activities from straight teaching to process consulting. Successful training programs require more than a text, audio visuals, and case studies. A skilled presenter, confident of the benefits of applying proactive skills to the job setting, can make a significant impact on an organization's ability to excel.

The role of process consultant requires a great deal of practice and help as a mentor or coach. Once prepared, the specialist can provide essential follow-up involvement within the organization, often making the critical difference in effective implementation of process skill development. A good example of how a process consultant can function with a group is presented in the following application example.

COMPUTER ASSISTED PLANNING

While hiding in the organizational library trying to finish a writing project, you are interrupted by your secretary asking you to accept an urgent call on your phone. With reluctance you agree to take it.

On the line is John Hardy, a computer specialist, who has attended several of your management development programs. He apologizes for interrupting you and tells you the following story:

> We are in the middle of a very important meeting. There are four of us here and we have already spent six hours trying to make progress on our problem. I don't know what's wrong. However, I think you can help.

The group is a task force that has been exploring the application of computer technology to production planning. Their activity to date has been a sixteen-city tour in North America seeking "state of the art theory and applications." This tour was taken by two members, Harry and Larry, from the production planning office. They visited universities, computer companies, and production planning departments in leading companies in the United States and Canada.

The current meeting is their first meeting after the trip. At the meeting are Harry, Larry, John, and Maxine. John and Maxine are the experts in computer technology in the company who have been advising the other two prior to the trips. Specifically, they have been trying to tell them who to see, what to look for, and what data to collect.

You agree to go and spend one hour to see if you can help them get sorted out. As you enter the room you see the following:

1. The room is a physical mess. Flip chart papers are on the wall, over chairs, files are strewn all over the tables, chairs, and the floor.
2. Physically they are seated as follows:

> Larry X   X John
> Harry X   X Maxine

They are at opposite ends of the room even though the table does not force the separation.

198

   3. John is banging the table and telling Harry and Larry that they have
           missed the whole point of visiting sixteen cities.

Your entry is greeted with sighs of relief from John and Maxine, whom you
know, and looks of disbelief from Harry and Larry. After introductions,
three of them begin to tell you what they see as the problem. With some
difficulty you finally create the following list:

   1. This meeting is unproductive and creating ill feelings.
   2. The problem has lost its identity in a mass of data.
   3. They don't know where to go from here.
   4. Management wants a report on the trip.
   5. They don't know whether computer-assisted planning is valid for
           their needs.
   6. A problem definitely exists.

All during the discussion constant interruptions occur correcting the story
told by the narrator.

   As you look at the flip charts, you discover that they have begun a
decision and have a decision title, "How best to introduce C.A.P. (Computer Assisted Planning)." Underneath this they have listed four methods of
introduction. These range from a totally integrated inventory control and
job card program to a simple computer status report retrieval system.

   Beside each alternative is a range of evaluative judgments, such as
"good," "not applicable," "too expensive."

   Ignoring all of this turmoil you try to determine why they are there.
After three false attempts, false because of the disagreements attached to
them, you finally ask, "Who has the problem?" Harry admits that he and
Larry have the problem and he sees it as follows:

> Sales has told us that our lead time from acceptance of order to delivery
> is too great. Even though we are in the custom design and development
> business, we still take two years to deliver. This involves the three key
> phases of preproduction:
>
>   1. Design specification and generation.
>   2. Engineering drawings.
>   3. Prototype development.

It is believed that C.A.P. might be helpful in solving their problem. A task
force was created and told to report on the feasibility of using some form of
C.A.P. John and Maxine were assigned as content experts to the task force.
John and Maxine are trying to force a decision from Harry and Larry. The
two production planning people are resisting because they don't have an

answer based on their tour. They need a trip report but don't know what to report.

There is obvious anxiety in the group because John and Maxine are talking about not being able to afford the time to go around on this one again, and they need some answers now.

Larry, who hasn't said a word since you entered the room, is heard to mutter, "I wonder how the 'guru' is going to handle this ego trip of John's."

What type of intervention would you use, and how would you go about it?

RESOLUTION

(This was an actual situation that occurred to one of our clients and the following is how it was resolved:)

The Process Consultant has a critical role of separating symptoms from causes. The group was obviously manifesting a wide range of symptoms. While some of the symptoms, for example, physical separation, name calling, and buck passing, had to be resolved, it was felt that the key intervention should be in the Decision Making Process.

The consultant began by testing the validity and appropriateness of the decision purpose through process development based intervention. As stated it was "How best to introduce Computer Assisted Planning to the orgnization?" The test questions that are covered in the chapter on Decision Making were used:

1. Why is this decision necessary?
2. What was the last decision made?

Within three minutes the group realized that the initial decision purpose was not the real issue facing the group. The decision of how to introduce Computer Assisted Planning (CAP) was precipitous. The key situation to resolve involved the extensive leadtime between the generation of product ideas and actual product development. After a few minutes of discussion the group developed a new statement, "How best to reduce the leadtime in product development?" Obviously Computer Assisted Planning was an alternative. Other options, such as increasing research staff and modifying research procedures, were also considered.

When the group was confident that they were addressing the right issue they dismissed the process consultant and were able to use the Decision Making Process. The ultimate decision was the introduction of a Computer Assisted Planning Process that included graphic terminals and computerized drafting practices. A minimum of six months has been reported to have been eliminated in the product development process. This includes the normal start-up problems. Estimates project that another three months will be saved as the software is improved.

Bibliography

Barnard, Chester L., *Functions of the Executive,* Harvard University Press, Cambridge, Mass., 1968.

Bross, Irwin J.D., *Design for Decision,* Free Press, New York, 1965.

Connonlly, F., *A Rhetoric Case Book,* Harcourt Brace, New York, 1953.

Drucker, Peter, *Managing for Results,* Harper & Row, New York, 1964.

Drucker, Peter, *Managing for Results,* Harper & Row, New York, 1964.

Emery, D., *The Compleat Manager,* McGraw-Hill, New York, 1978.

Kepner, C. H., B. B. Tregoe, *The Rational Manager,* McGraw-Hill, New York, 1965.

Miller, Gordon and Henry Mintzberg, *Normative Models in Management Decision-Making,* Society of Industrial Accountants, 1975.

Mintzberg, H., *The Nature of Managerial Work,* Harper & Row, New York, 1977.

Plato, *The Republic,* Modern Library, New York, 1934.

Plunkett, L. and G. Hale, *Process Management Skills,* Alamo Publishing, Alamo, Calif., 1979.

Rachlis, H., *Clear Thinking,* Harper & Row, New York, 1962.

Richards, M., *Management: Decisions & Behaviour,* Paul Greenlow, Richard Irwin, Inc., Toronto, Canada, 1972.

Russel, Bertrand, *A History of Western Philosophy,* Simon & Schuster, New York, 1945.

Samuel, Herbert, *Essay in Physics,* Harcourt Brace, New York, 1952.

Schein, Edgar, *Process Consultation,* Addison Wesley, Reading, Mass., 1960.

Simon, H., *Administrative Behaviour,* Free Press, New York, 1976.

Stryker, Perrin, "Can You Analyse This Problem?" *Harvard Business Review,* May–June, 1965.

Stryker, Perrin, "How to Analyse That Problem," *Harvard Business Review,* July–August, 1965.

Glossary

Action Plan.   The determination of the most appropriate analytical tool for the resolution of a concern.

Adaptive Action.   An action taken to permit an ability to live with or accommodate to certain effects. Where no corrective action is possible it might be necessary to cope.

Alarm Trigger.   A predetermined state of affairs that dictates the need to activate a contingent action.

Alternative Comparison.   The process of cross-referencing the alternative recommendations against predetermined factors to assess relative performance.

Causal Chain.   The listing in chronological sequence of causes and effects in direct relationship.

Cause.   The verifiable event that can be attributed to creating a described effect.

Comparable Facts.   The listing of key facts that are used for creating a tight boundary around the observed effects. These are used for comparison to create differences or clues for causal development.

Concern.   Any set of events, data, or actual or perceived occurrences that indicates to a manager the need to act or analyze.

Contingent Action.   An action that is preplanned to provide protection by minimizing the effect of a potential problem if it occurs. A contingent action can also be used to maximize the effect of a potential opportunity.

Corrective Action.   An action aimed at removing the proven cause of a variance and thus returning the performance to its standard level.

Critical Areas.   Those areas within a plan that require further analysis to guarantee optimum results.

Decision Criteria.   A list of those criteria that will influence the selection of an alternative. This list will normally include a statement of specified end results and statements of resource limitations.

Decision Purpose.   A statement of intended result expected as a result of the decision.

Desirables.   Factors whose presence is desirable but not mandatory for a decision.

Destructive Testing.   The process of logically forcefitting possible causes through the variance description to assess probability.

Differences.   These are the product of comparing what was observed with what was not observed. Key differences are critical for developing causes.

Effect.   An observable and describable event, or set of events or behaviors that can be either undesirable, desirable, or neutral.

Facilitative Action.   A preplanned activity that is aimed at increasing the probability of the occurrence of a likely cause.

Final Choice.   The recommendation that performs best against the Decision Criteria and has the most acceptable degree of risk.

Growth Potential.   The assessment of potential growth trend of a concern to assess priority.

Impact.   The description of the current effect of a concern in an attempt to set priority.

Interim Action.   An action taken to gain time for an in-depth analysis. It relieves effects for a short time.

Likely Causes.   The listing of potential causes that can be manipulated to increase or decrease the probability of occurrence.

Limits.   A predetermined requirement for a decision that must be complied with absolutely for the ultimate appropriateness of the decision.

Observed Facts.   The description of the key facts used in defining or specifying a variance or undesirable effect.

Plan Statement.   The specific statement of a plan's end result.

Possible Causes.   A list of hypotheses or theories derived from experience, changes, or distinctive features that could possibly explain the variance.

Potential Opportunities.   Those desirable effects which could occur, enhancing the ultimate success of a plan.

Potential Problems.   Those undesirable effects which could exist, and interfere with a plan's ultimate success.

Preventive Action.   A preplanned activity that is aimed at reducing the probability of the occurrence of a likely cause.

Probable Cause.   That possible cause which best survives the destructive test and best explains the facts as described.

Risk Analysis.   The process of generating and assessing risk to provide an added data input for ultimate choice recommendation.

Risk Assessment.   The process of applying evaluative measures of probability and seriousness to increase our ability to understand risk.

Risk Generation.   The process of listing possible adverse effects of a tentative recommendation. This listing is based on experience.

Separation.   The process of reducing concerns to an analyzable level of management; the breaking down of generalized concerns.

Set Priority.   The establishment of a hierarchy based on importance.

Tentative Choice.   The recommendation that seems to provide the best performance when evaluated against the Decision Criteria.

Urgency.   The description of target dates or time parameters that influence priority.

Appendix

THE ALAMO CONSULTING GROUP, INC.

Walnut Creek, California

The concepts and skills taught in this book have been developed, structured, and refined by the authors and their associates at The Alamo Consulting Group of Walnut Creek, California. The Alamo Consulting Group is in the business of delivering professional management development programs to a variety of companies in problem solving, decision making, and planning skills.

The programs delivered by Alamo are designed essentially for three different groups within an organization. *The Process Management Skills* (PMS) program is targeted to middle and top management and includes Cause Analysis, Decision Making, and Plan Analysis.

The second program is specifically for supervisors and key nonmanagement people. This program is entitled *Analytical Problem Solving* (APS). We subscribe to the philosophy that the tools for problem solving should be provided for those individuals in an organization who have already had exposure to problems and have the data for effective resolutions. Therefore, APS emphasizes the Cause Analysis Process and concentrates on solving real problems faced in a company. The program is taught on the company premises where the individuals in the seminars participate in teams of three or four people and gather data on current equipment, production, or systems problems.

During the APS program, many problems are actually resolved. After a problem has been "fixed," a person from the client company documents the actual cost savings of the "fix" to the company. Many of our clients experience very dramatic results from the APS program. One client has estimated that since implementing APS the company has saved over $3,000,000 as a direct result of the program.

The third program that Alamo delivers is called *Trouble Shooting Skills for the Service Representative.* This program was originally developed for companies in the electronics industry that have large organizations of service representatives who are responsible for servicing the electronic hardware and software that they have installed in their client's facilities. Many electronics companies are very effective at training their service representatives in the engineering aspects of solving problems, but do not have a systematic trouble shooting process for dealing with problems throughout their organization.

Alamo not only provides a systematic training program for solving real service-oriented problems, we also work with our clients to develop a trouble shooting management system to be used throughout a service organization. For example, we have helped clients develop such tools as call report forms all the way up to developing an internal communication system to inform all service representatives in a company about solutions being developed in other geographical locations. This program is now expanded for use in other kinds of service organizations outside of the electronics industry.

The Alamo Consulting Group has three different ways to deliver the programs described above:

1. *Public Seminars.* At least once a month in some part of the world Alamo will have a seminar open to the public.
2. *Private Sessions.* On request from our clients, Alamo will conduct seminars exclusively for a company at a location of the client's choice. The number of people in a private seminar is usually limited to 20 participants.
3. *Licensing Instructors.* Alamo will train a company's own instructors to deliver the programs internally within their organization. In order to be certified as instructors, individuals must go through a regular program, complete a one-week Alamo Instructor Development (AID) program, and then co-teach their first session with an Alamo professional instructor. Once this process has been completed, the instructor is certified to teach either *Process Management Skills, Analytical Problem Solving,* or *Trouble Shooting Skills for the Service Representative* using the Alamo training materials.

All of the seminars are three days in length. The seminars are modularized and can be given in half-day- or one-day-a-week programs lasting three weeks. The structuring and determining of how a program can best meet a client's needs are worked out in every case individually with a client before the program is implemented. Modifications and customization plans are determined with the company's trainer in the *Alamo Instructor Development* program.

As a complement to the structured approach to Problem Solving, Decision Making, and Planning, the Alamo Consulting Group also conducts training in creative problem solving through a course called *Criteria Optimization Techniques* (COT). In-depth seminars in this innovative process are delivered on the same basis as the other programs. The optimum implementation would be for the COT Process to follow the structured process training as complementary developmental programs for managers.

The Alamo Consulting Group also provides training in *Presentation Skills* for managers and salespersons and in the *Consultative Approach to Selling*, designed specifically for the professional salesperson.

CAUSE ANALYSIS WORKSHEET

STEP 1. State Problem (include object and defect):Deer Highway (extension)

STEP 2. Describe Problem (good questions = good facts)	Observed Facts	Comparative Facts
What • On what object is the defect observed? • What exactly is wrong (defect)?	• Deer Highway (extension) • potholes	• all other major highways in D4 (map) Capitol/ Deer Hwy. South, Salmon/ Black Bear Hwy.)
Where • Where is the object with the defect observed (geographically)? • Where on the object does the defect appear?	• River City to Pepperly • entire surface, mostly right-hand lanes	• buckles, cracked, sinking • River City to southern border • over entire surface evenly
When • When was defect first observed (clock/calendar time)? • When in the lifetime of the object was the defect first observed? • In what pattern is the defect observed?	• mid December '80 • 2½ years old, winter season • continually recurring since Dec.	• Aug. '79 to mid Dec. '80 • immediately after opening or whenever reasonable • periodic, non-recurring
Magnitude • How much of the object is defective? • How many objects are defective? • What is the trend?	• maximum 20 potholes 1 mile • up to 36" across and 16" deep • increasing	• more or less • bigger/smaller • decreasing

OPTIONAL STEP. Examine and Test Experiential Causes

Figure A.1 Sample Resolution

STEP 3. Identify Differences	STEP 4. List Changes	STEP 5. and 6. Generate Likely Causes and Test
• built on landfill • last major new road construction in D4 • Deer River runs beside it	• N/C • resurfaced early summer '80 • more water in river since 11/80	1. heavy rains, water seeps under road and creates potholes • doesn't explain object
• closer to earthquake center • demonstration 9/80 • heavy traffic/assumption missile carriers & convoys	• event after Xmas '80 • increased rocket testing	2. resurfacing material • ? object
• draught ended • first winter after resurfacing	• heavy rains mid 11/80	3. road built on landfill coupled with change in weather (heavy rains) • fits all facts

STEP 7. Verify Most Likely Cause

- Rain with landfill causes potholes. Road built on landfill coupled with change in weather (heavy rains) fits all facts.
- Go back and review engineering spec's for landfill; talk to construction company.

of the Riverside Case.

STANDARD DECISION MAKING WORKSHEET

STEP 1. State Decision Purpose: Select best method for disposing of "Insurance" Fund

STEP 2. Establish Decision Criteria	STEP 3. Separate Criteria	
• Dispose of entire fund • Dispose of fund within 12 mos. • Reflect needs of retired • High state-wide visibility • Cost the tax payers nothing extra • Positive impact on Governor's party • Positive impact on Commission image	**Limits** • Dispose of entire fund • Dispose of fund within 12 mos.	
	Desirables	**Value**
	• Have positive impact on Governor's party	10
	• High state-wide visibility	9
	• Cost tax payers nothing extra	8
	• Reflect needs of retired	6
	• Positive impact on Commission image	4

STEP 6. and 7. Identify and Assess Risk (note probability and seriousness)

Alternative B	P / S	
• If: People who hadn't been residents get the rebate money • Then: Previous residents will become unhappy • If: • Then:	5	3

Figure A.2 Sample Resolution of the

STEP 4. and 5. Generate and Compare Alternatives

(Alternate A) Limits	Go/ No Go	(Alternate B) Limits	Go/ No Go	(Alternate C) Limits	Go/ No Go
• 6 months	GO	• 1 year	GO	• 12 months	GO
• $12,000,000	GO	• $12,000,000	GO	• $12,000,000	GO

Desirables	Score/ Wt. Score	**Desirables**	Score/ Wt. Score	**Desirables**	Score/ Wt. Score
• Increase quality of commission service	6 | 60	• Returned tax revenue looks good	80 | 80	• If disaster minimized, could look good	10 | 100
• Benefits all equally who use service	5 | 45	• Benefits all utility users	10 | 90	• Probably recieve much press coverage	9 | 81
• Utilize only existing monies	10 | 80	• Utilize only existing monies	10 | 80	• Uses all money to launch/may cost on-going revenue	7 | 56
• Benefits all equally who use	4 | 24	• Elderly get tax return	10 | 60	• Only in the event of emergency or disaster	8 | 48
• Increase quality of commission image	8 | 32	• Commission shows tax payers its interest in them	10 | 40	• High publicity	8 | 32
Total 241		**Total** 350		**Total** 317	

STEP 6. and 7. (continued)

Alternative C	P / S
• If: There are no "visible" disasters in the next few years • Then: The Satelite system may not have high positive visibility— giving the impression that it just costs money. • If: • Then:	6 | 8

Corporation Commission Case.

PLAN ANALYSIS WORKSHEET

STEP 1. State the Plan Briefly (end result desired):Successfully introduce and orient Don Cameron to Velex Laboratories

STEP 2. List/Review Steps in Plan and Indicate Critical Areas			**STEP 3.** Identify Potential Problems/Opportunities (probability and seriousness of priorities)		**STEP 4.** Determine Likely Causes of Key Potential Problems/Opportunities
Agenda Item	Date	By Whom		P/S	
Visit to lab in basement to meet research techs and view equipment.					
1. Memo to lab re: visit/ one week prior.					
• assign lab member to orient Don re: current and future projects			• Absence of lab member		• Sick • Family Problems
2. Routing					
• meet Southern & Don at service elevators 3 lab tech heads 10:30am					
• tour of labs #1, 2, 3, in order until 11:15 am orientation by member			• Don can't hear orientation by lab member		• Don has hearing problem and soft spoken orientator • Noisy lab
• restroom break/conversation 11:15am					
3. 11:30 am depart service area—back upstairs.					

Figure A.3   Sample Resolution

214

STEP 5. Develop Preventive/Facilitative Action(s)	STEP 6. Plan Contingent Action(s)	STEP 7. Build In Alarms to Trigger Contingent Action(s)
• Megavitamins • No action	• Second staff member prepared and ready	• Southern calls first staff member at 8:30 am
• Alert orientator to speak loudly • Shut down lab	• Provide Don with written outline of presentation	• Indications (nonverbal) from Don that he doesn't hear (Southern checks)

of the Velex Laboratories Case.

Index